DR YESHAYAHU (JESAIAH
spiritual scientist, philosophe
—is founder of the anthropo.
in Harduf, Israel, co-founder of the Global
Network for Social Threefolding, director of
Global Event College and contributor to the School
of Spiritual Science. He is the author of *Cognitive
Yoga, Jerusalem, The Twilight and Resurrection of Humanity, Spiritual
Science in the 21st Century, The Spiritual Event of the Twentieth Century,
The Event in Science, History, Philosophy & Art, The New Experience of
the Supersensible, America's Global Responsibility* and *Cognitive Yoga:
How a Book is Born.*

THE THREE MEETINGS

Christ, Michael and Anthroposophia

Prelude to the new edition of
The New Experience of the Supersensible

Yeshayahu (Jesaiah) Ben-Aharon

TEMPLE LODGE

Temple Lodge Publishing Ltd.
Hillside House, The Square
Forest Row, RH18 5ES

www.templelodge.com

First published by Temple Lodge Publishing, 2022

© Yeshayahu Ben-Aharon 2022

The Publishers are grateful to Scott Hicks for his editorial support

This book is copyright under the Berne Convention. All rights reserved. Apart from any fair dealing for the purpose of private study, research, criticism or review, no part of this publication may be reproduced, stored in a retrieval system, or transmitted in any form or by any means, electronic, electrical, chemical, mechanical, optical, photocopying, recording or otherwise, without the prior written permission of the copyright owner. Inquiries should be addressed to the Publishers

The right of Yeshayahu Ben-Aharon to be identified as the author of this work has been asserted in accordance with sections 77 and 78 of the Copyright, Designs and Patents Act, 1988

A CIP catalogue record for this book is available from the British Library

ISBN 978 1 912230 91 4

Cover by Morgan Creative
Typeset by Symbiosys Technologies, Vishakapatnum, India
Printed by 4Edge Ltd., Essex

Contents

Preface

The unsolvable question with which Thomas Aquinas died was 'How does the Christ enter human thinking? How will human thinking be Christened? ... This question stands in world history when Thomas Aquinas died in 1274. Up to this moment he could only advance to this question, which stands there with all heartfelt inwardness in European spiritual culture'.[1] A century earlier the same question, 'with all heartfelt inwardness', confronted Alanus ab Insulis, the leading Platonist of Chartres, as can be seen from his book, *The Rhythm of the Incarnation of Christ*.[2] The unresolved question of Thomas and Alanus was answered by Rudolf Steiner in *The Philosophy of Freedom* in 1894, the fountainhead of modern spiritual science. At the end of the twentieth century, the question resounded strongly again, in this form: 'How does the etheric Christ enter spiritual science?' This question stood there in world history when Rudolf Steiner died in 1925. Up to that moment anthroposophy could only advance as far as this question, which stands there with all heartfelt inwardness in humanity's spiritual culture.

In my early 20s, the new Damascus event, which Rudolf Steiner predicted, was for me a given supersensible fact. So was also the physical form of anthroposophy. It was clear to me that without the light of spiritual science, the meeting with the etheric Christ only remains a personal experience. And without the new life forces streaming from the etheric Christ, anthroposophy remains a physical body of knowledge; both need each other. The new Christ event must be investigated by spiritual science to become known to humanity, and anthroposophy requires His life forces to be born again. I confronted this question with the greatest intensity: How does the etheric Christ enter spiritual science? To gain spiritual-scientific knowledge of the etheric Christ and bring about a resurrection of anthroposophy became my daily spiritual work. But a path had first to be created, to bring about the reciprocal relations between them.

---

[1] Rudolf Steiner, lecture of 23 May 1920 (GA 74). See list of Rudolf Steiner's works on p. 140.

[2] *Rhythmus über die Inkarnation Christi*, translated from the Latin *Rhythmus de incarnatione Christi* by Wilhelm Rath (*Die Drei*, 1951/3).

The first glimpse of an answer to this question was found when I read *The Philosophy of Freedom* for the first time. I felt that it let me breathe freely with the Christ experience and anthroposophy and allowed me to bring them increasingly together. The activity of thinking stimulated by *The Philosophy of Freedom* produced a spiritual light that illuminated the Christ experience and resurrected anthroposophy and established an initial bridge between them. With the living light of *The Philosophy of Freedom*, I felt that I could work towards the goal of wedding anthroposophy with the etheric Christ, and it proved to be the beginning of the path that in the coming years and decades would increasingly let the forces of the etheric Christ enter into spiritual science.

The question was also formulated by Rudolf Steiner in 1917 in this way: 'How can we prepare our souls to draw near to the Christ whose presence will be experienced in the etheric world in the present century? What steps must we take, especially in our present age, to draw near to Him?'[3] Today, it must be rephrased accordingly: 'How can our souls unite with the etheric Christ, experienced in the etheric world, since the end of last century? What steps must we take, in the second century of the Age of Michael, to unite with Him?'

In the first edition of *The New Experience of the Supersensible*, published in 1995, I called the path developed to answer this question, 'the knowledge drama of the Second Coming'. As I am presently preparing the new edition of this book after 30 years, I have realized that it must become a greatly expanded work. I wrote *The Three Meetings* as a prelude, to introduce the new edition of *The New Experience of the Supersensible* in a form that may also be more accessible to a greater circle of readers.

---

[3] Lecture of 17 April 1917 (GA 175).

Introduction

At the centre of the evolution of humanity and the earth stands the Mystery of Golgotha, through which the Christ impulse entered the earth. Rudolf Steiner pointed out that anthroposophy was given at the beginning of the last century to prepare for the second major Christ event in human evolution, the etheric Second Coming that began in 1933. As a result of the history of the twentieth century, described in *The Twilight and Resurrection of Humanity*, the Second Coming was reversed into its evil opposite on earth. After the death of Rudolf Steiner in 1925, anthroposophy was disconnected from the new revelation of the Christ and the developing stream of Michael, and this separation continued until the end of the century. The meetings with the etheric Christ, Michael and Anthroposophia, described in this book, as a Prelude to the second edition of *The New Experience of the Supersensible*, are possible because of the Second Coming. It is the portal that leads to the mighty and transformative events that are taking place in the etheric world right now in the present age.

We must distinguish between two aspects of the meeting with the etheric Christ in the modern Christ experience. The first is that the meeting with the etheric Christ in the etheric world is a gift of grace. It is initiated and given to man by the Christ. Rudolf Steiner emphasized that there is a 'tremendous difference' between this meeting and the way an initiate perceives the Christ voluntarily in the spiritual world:

> There is a tremendous difference between what trained clairvoyants experience and what is described here as something that will come about in the natural course of events. Since time immemorial the trained clairvoyant experienced the Christ by means of certain exercises. On the physical plane, if I meet a man, he is there is front of me; with clairvoyant vision I can perceive him in quite different places, and we do not actually meet. It has always been possible to see the Christ clairvoyantly. But to meet Him, now that He stands in a different relationship to humanity, in other words, that He helps us from out of the etheric world, is something which is independent of our clairvoyant development. From the twentieth century onwards, in the next

three thousand years, certain people will be able to meet Him,
meet Him objectively as an etheric form. That is very different
from experiencing a vision of Him through inner development. [4]

This meeting is an expression of the fact that today the Christ 'stands
in a different relationship to humanity', and 'He helps us from out
of the etheric world'. In other words, in this meeting we meet the
Christ as 'if I meet a man', and therefore the Christ 'is there in front
of me'. This is therefore a *meeting face to face*, like the way we meet
another person in the physical world face to face. In such meetings,
we perceive and experience the being of the Christ directly, and its
impression encompasses all levels and aspects of our human constitution and existence.

This is the first aspect of the meeting, which is experienced as a
given gift of grace, that does not require previous spiritual knowledge. But it can become a starting point of spiritual-scientific development, that leads to a second meeting gained in a voluntary way.
In this case, as in Parsifal's path to the Grail, we must distinguish
between the *first* meeting, which is given as a gift of grace, and
the *second* meeting, that was gained through conscious spiritual
development. *The New Experience of the Supersensible*, Chapter 4,
describes the given meeting, and Chapter 5 describes the second
meeting gained through voluntary spiritual development.

The second, voluntary, meeting with the Christ was described by
Rudolf Steiner in the following way:

> If souls allow spiritual science to kindle understanding of such
> secrets, they become fit to recognize in that Holy Chalice the
> Mystery of the Christ-'I,' the eternal 'I' which every human 'I'
> can become. The secret is a reality—only human beings must
> allow themselves to be summoned through spiritual science
> to understand this, in order that as they contemplate the Holy
> Grail, the Christ-'I' may be received into their being... when
> human beings are better prepared to receive the Christ Ego, then
> it will pour in greater and greater fullness into their souls. They
> will then evolve to the level of Christ Jesus, their great Example.
> Then for the first time they will learn to understand the sense in
> which Christ Jesus is the Great Example for humanity. [5]

---

[4] Lecture of 17 September 1911 (GA 130).
[5] Lecture of 11 April 1909 (GA 109).

In another lecture Rudolf Steiner emphasizes the timely nature of this process:

> Yes, these imprinted copies of the Christ Jesus individuality are waiting to be taken in by human souls—they are waiting! [6]

The path from the first, given meeting with the Christ to the second meeting, in which we actualize a conscious reception of His 'I', is the path of the knowledge drama of the Second Coming. Its aim is to transform the gift of the given meeting into a fully conscious reception and individualization of His 'I' copy. But the more we develop the path that leads to the voluntary second meeting and the reception of Christ's 'I', we realize that its spiritual seed was implicit in the first, given, meeting. When the given meeting is transformed into the voluntary meeting, we realize that the copy of Christ's 'I', that we receive and individualize consciously, was contained in the being of the Christ that we experienced in the first meeting. The knowledge drama of the Second Coming leads us to 'contemplate the Holy Grail' in order that 'the Christ-"I" may be received into the human being'. Then we discover, in the light of spiritual knowledge, radiating from the Holy Grail, that the Christ Himself is the source of the copies of His 'I'. We 'recognize in that Holy Chalice the Mystery of the Christ-"I," the eternal "I" which every human "I" can become', and through the knowledge drama, we actively participate in this becoming.

For this reason, the gracefully given meeting with the etheric Christ must be understood not as a finished single event, but as the planting of a fiery spiritual seed of His 'I' in the human spirit, soul, and body. Modern spiritual science offers the required spiritual knowledge and practice, to fully receive and individualize the given seed of the Christ-'I'. This event is only the start of a lifelong, indeed, eternal process of spiritual becoming. In the words cited above, Rudolf Steiner emphasizes the *gradual* nature of this process. 'The Christ-"I"... will imbue the souls of human beings to an *ever-increasing degree* so that they can strive upward to approach the position where their great model Christ Jesus used to be'. We should add to the image of 'the "I" *copy*' used by Rudolf Steiner, also the image of the *seed*. What happens to this seed after its graceful giving depends entirely on our free spiritual activity. The gradual

---

[6] Lecture of 7 March 1909 (GA 109).

process of spiritual growth and development that began in a singular event of grace, is a seed planted in the fertile spiritual soil of human hearts and through the sunlight of modern spiritual knowledge it can develop and bear much fruit.

When the true nature of the first and second, given and voluntary, meetings with the Christ is fully grasped, we can say with Rudolf Steiner, that in truth 'it is the Christ that gives me my humanity'.[7] This means that in our age, through the etheric Second Coming, it becomes possible for more and more people to prepare themselves to receive the Ego-copy of the Christ, and say, 'looking up to Christ, let there always stand in our soul: *Christ is the archetype of the "I"; let my "I" strive to become a copy of this archetype'*.[8]

[7] *Leading Thoughts*, 'The Mission of Michael in the Cosmic Age of Human Freedom' (GA 26).
[8] Esoteric lesson of 3 March 1909 (GA 266). My italics.

Chapter 1
The Ur-Phenomena of the Modern Christ Experience

Paul's Christ Experience and the Birth of Christian Platonism

Rudolf Steiner's spiritual investigations have shown that Paul's experience at the gates of Damascus is an archetype of the experience of the etheric Christ in the Second Coming, that will become increasingly possible for more people starting from the 1930s and 1940s and in the coming 3000 years.[9]

The unique nature of Paul's experience was that it combined three streams together, in a wholly new spiritual synthesis. First, Paul received the gift of the *new* spiritual faculties, that allowed him to experience the etheric Christ as a given event. For humanity, these faculties could only begin to appear after 1933. Second, Paul was thoroughly schooled in the Greek and Roman philosophy of his time. And third, he was also an 'initiate of the old Cabala' prior to this experience.[10] Therefore, it was his pioneering task to unite these three into one stream, spiritualized by the new Christ impulse. His mission was to form out of the three the new synthesis of the Christian path of initiation, which takes into full consideration the fact that, beginning with Plato and Aristotle, the cosmic sun intelligence was descending to the earth, following the incarnation of Christ, and departing from the hands of Michael. This synthesis was Paul's original spiritual creation. That is, the Pauline, consciously investigated Christ experience is the first—and archetypal—example of the self-conscious and free, active reciprocal connection between a given Christ experience, active thinking, and the principle of initiation, which together make possible clear and precise spiritual knowledge of Christ. The same synthesis must be achieved also today, by means of our individual spiritual activity, through modern spiritual science.

---

[9] Most of Rudolf Steiner's lectures about the etheric Second Coming are collected in GA 118 and GA 130.

[10] Lecture of 31 May 1909 (GA 109/111).

The source of Paul's spiritual creation is the same source today as it was 2000 years ago, because it is the etheric Christ Himself that is the source of this creation. Our task is to bring all the forces of the Consciousness Soul, through spiritual science, to meet the etheric Christ, to investigate the conscious modern meeting with the Christ, as Paul did with the forces of the Mind Soul in the fourth post-Atlantean age.

Rudolf Steiner characterized Paul's unique creation, that he calls the 'Pauline method', in this way:

> The first who could perceive the cosmic significance of the Christ was Paul, who could perceive how the power of Christ's being streamed into the aura of the Earth. That which was grasped by Paul as a specific point of the knowledge of Christ can, if we deepen the occultism of our time, be grasped by man in wider fields of Christ knowledge. If the vision of Paul ... be extended from what for Paul was almost only the perception of Jesus Christ, to the life of Jesus Christ as a whole, then *the Pauline method* will be extended from a single centre over the total event of Jesus Christ's life. If today we can reach the position, by means of devoted occult research, *making the Pauline method a general method of Christ knowledge,* a real advance in the knowledge of the Christ will have occurred.[11]

For those who strive today to form an individualized 'Pauline method' to investigate the modern Damascus event, this indication is of great importance, because it connects the Damascus event to the fundamental problems and tasks of gaining spiritual-scientific knowledge, in the physical and spiritual worlds. This becomes immediately clear when Rudolf Steiner points out that the first problem encountered by Paul, because of his Christ experience, was the question about the true nature of human thinking:

> So Paul came to realize that an enemy attacked human evolution, and that this enemy is the source of error on the Earth ... Only in a world in which the human being could be influenced by the Ahrimanic forces—so Paul now felt—could the

---

[11] Lecture of 27 May 1914 (GA 152). My italics. The 'Pauline method' as practiced by Rudolf Steiner, is the foundation of the knowledge drama of the Second Coming.

error occur that led to the death on the cross. And now, when he understood this, he realized for the first time the truth of esoteric Christianity. *The assimilation of death into life: this is the secret of Golgotha.* Previously man knew life without death; now he learned to know death as part of life, as an experience that strengthens life ... Humanity must strengthen its life, if it wants to pass through death and yet live. And death means, in this connection ... the intellect ... the intellect makes us inwardly cold, makes us inwardly dead. The intellect paralyses us. Man must truly feel it, that man lives not when man thinks; that man wastes his life in dead mental pictures, and that man must have strong life in himself to feel creative life in the dead mental pictures ... This I tried to do in my *Philosophy of Freedom*. This *Philosophy of Freedom* is a moral conception that should be a preparation for the vitalization of dead thinking through moral impulse, to bring it to resurrection.[12]

And further:

> What Paul meant by the resurrected Christ was that the Christ experienced death, but that He overcame death, that He as a spiritual-living triumphant being came forth out of death in the resurrection and that He lives since then with humanity, that without Christ man would have had only dead thinking ... Whereas before, in former times, thinking still carried its living essence into earthly life, since the third and fourth centuries ... the earthly human soul can awaken its thinking through the direct beholding of the Mystery of Golgotha.[13]

---

[12] Lecture of 2 April 1922 (GA 211). My italics. In the nineteenth century the death process of thinking had reached a further, mighty acceleration: 'The Fall into sin ... influenced at last the intellect as well. The intellect felt itself [in the nineteenth century] at the limits of knowledge. And if the theologians speak about sin, or Du Bois-Reymond speaks about the limits of knowledge of nature, it is the same, only in somewhat different form.' (GA 220, lecture of 21 January 1923.) The second Mystery of Golgotha that started at the end of the nineteenth century, described in Chapters 4 and 5 of *The New Experience of the Supersensible*, has its roots in this intellectual second Fall of man.

[13] Lecture of 15 April 1922 (GA 211).

Naturally, when Rudolf Steiner speaks about *The Philosophy of Freedom* in connection with the 'Pauline method', 'epistemology' or 'theory of knowledge', he doesn't use these terms in the ordinary philosophical sense. Rudolf Seiner and Paul are spiritual scientists, not mere thinkers, and therefore both consider the spiritualization of thinking as the first stage of acquiring empirical supersensible knowledge. *The Philosophy of Freedom* is not an ordinary philosophic book as it is often taken to be. It is as empirical and scientific as any other anthroposophical book or lecture of Rudolf Steiner's, and if we experience it as such, we will experience through thinking that we participate in a living spiritual reality, and we will be able not only to understand the communications from the higher worlds, but also experience the reality of such communications, because we already experienced real spiritual life *through* pure and intuitive thinking.

'The secret of esoteric Christianity: the assimilation of death into life', which was Paul's most significant discovery 2000 years ago, is also the fundamental discovery made in the present meeting with the etheric Christ. Overcoming the death forces inherent in the modern ahrimanic intellect is indeed the starting point for the knowledge drama of the Second Coming, presented in Chapter 5 of *The New Experience of the Supersensible*, outlined below. And the source of the forces of resurrection that make the overcoming of death possible, is found in the appearance, words, and deeds of the etheric Christ. Therefore, this is also the source of our search for a current 'Pauline method' to bring the present Christ event into spiritual science. For this purpose, we must direct our spiritual observation and investigation, as Paul did, to the being of Christ Himself.

Rudolf Steiner pointed out that the Christ incarnated in the Nathanic Jesus, which is the same being that incorporated itself in Krishna. This means that the being that created and inspired the Oriental yoga stream from immemorial times is the same being in which the Christ incarnated in Palestine. This knowledge has proved to be of greatest importance to our work. This mystery is revealed today when we investigate the etheric appearance of the Christ. In this meeting, we discover how ancient yoga was Christianized, and with it, the whole stream of Western thinking, in all its Platonic, Neo-Platonic and Aristotelian variations. It is here that we discover the inner link between the Pauline method of investigating the Christ experience and the first form of the

Michaelic Yoga practice. It originated in Paul's supersensible meeting with the Christ, and it repeats itself in each meeting. Its source is to be found in the light-radiating, life-giving spiritual aura of the Christ, the Nathanic-Krishna Being, in which the Christ is clothed also today.

It was the same Krishna-Nathanic-Jesus being who taught both Arjuna and Paul—the one before and the other after the Mystery of Golgotha—the secrets of Egohood, self-consciousness and its spiritualization. 'The spirit that works through Krishna appears again in the Jesus-child of St Luke, out of the Nathan line of the house of King David. This personality bore, in essence, everything that exists as impulses for the emancipation of man, for the release from external reality.'[14] This was the most mature pre-Golgotha form of the appearance of the primal Adam-Nathanic being of heavenly humanity, that became the vehicle for the Christ. Krishna renewed in this way the essence of ancient yoga and connected it with the Christ. 'He who spoke to the learned men in the Temple [when Jesus was twelve] was therefore not only Zarathustra speaking as an Ego, but one who spoke from those sources from which Krishna at one time drew yoga; he spoke of yoga raised a stage higher; he united himself with the Krishna force, with Krishna himself, in order to continue to grow until his thirtieth year.' Because 'he spoke of yoga raised a stage higher', when he united with the Christ in the Baptism by John in the Jordan River, he could, after the Mystery of Golgotha, reveal yoga's new essence to Paul. 'As Paul journeyed to Damascus it was the Christ who appeared before him. The light-appearance in which the Christ clothed Himself was Krishna. And because the Christ used Krishna as His own soul-sheath, through which He then continued to work, His radiance contains everything that once was the sublime content of the *Bhagavad-Gita* ... the teaching of Krishna became thereby a thing that belongs to the whole of humanity'.[15]

This is a most significant fact that remained unnoticed, that the new Michaelic Yoga draws its substance and forces from the Nathanic-Krishna being. But this is simply a fact of the modern Damascus event, and this is the reason why this book, which

---

[14] Lecture of 5 June 1913 (GA 146).
[15] Lecture of 1 January 1913 (GA 142).

describes this event, had to be based on the new Michaelic Yoga, because it is Michael who draws our attention to the fact that 'His radiance contains everything that once was the sublime content of the *Bhagavad-Gita*'. This light shines today as the new light of the Grail, in view of which the Ego of Christ is given to man by the Christ during the knowledge drama of the Second Coming.

This is really the reason why, when we perceive the etheric Christ as He appears again today in His radiant light aura, the Christ appears, speaks, and acts as the source and teacher of the new Michaelic Yoga of soul and spirit breathing. This is simply an etheric fact, grasped directly by means of imaginative perception, revealed in the rhythmical etheric life and light of Christ's new etheric appearance. This means that the source of the modern form of yoga, in its anthroposophical-Michaelic form, described by Rudolf Steiner in 1919-1920, is the etheric appearance of the Christ, because in this experience one becomes part of this new etheric breathing with one's etheric body, and one learns to develop and regulate this etheric breathing consciously, through the etherization of thinking and sense-perception, as described in some detail in *Cognitive Yoga: Making Yourself a New Etheric Body and Individuality*.[16]

In this manner we also resurrect today, on the etheric level of the Second Coming, the origin and development of Christian Platonism. The living esoteric stream of Platonic and Neo-Platonic Christianity began to flow in Paul's Damascus experience. The modern Damascus experience that began at the end of the twentieth century, brings about the Michaelic resurrection and transformation of this 2000-year-old stream. We feel ourselves embedded in this stream now, and we are conscious of the fact that we experience its resurrection and new beginning, on a higher level, transformed and spiritualized through the knowledge drama of the Second Coming. At the cusp of the transition from the second to the third millennium, old anthroposophy was resurrected and transformed through Christ's etheric appearance in His Second Coming, as the mysteries of Eleusis' and Plato's philosophy were resurrected and transformed by Paul's Christ experience at the gates of Damascus. In this way, the First and Second Comings, the first and second Mysteries of Golgotha, are connected today in the new impulse of Michael in the twenty-first century.

---

[16] Temple Lodge, 2016.

Two thousand years ago, in the esoteric school that Dionysius the Areopagite, the pupil of Paul, founded in Athens, the two sun streams were connected for the first time on the earth: the Christ that descended to the earth from the sun in the Mystery of Golgotha, beginning His activity in the spiritual aura of the earth, and the sun stream of Michael's cosmic intelligence descending after Him to become human thinking. Through Paul and Dionysius, the Platonic stream of Greek thinking, still connected to the Mysteries of Eleusis, was united for the first time with the Christ, and this united stream continued to spiritualize the evolution of thinking in Europe until Rudolf Steiner transformed it into modern spiritual science in *The Philosophy and Freedom* at the beginning of the new Age of Michael. And our central task since the end of the twentieth century is to unite Rudolf Steiner's creation to the etheric appearance of the Christ, making anthroposophy in the twenty-first century into a revelation of Christ's new appearance. Let us, therefore, briefly survey the main stages of the development of this united Michaelic-Christian, earthly-human sun impulse in the last 2000 years.

In the esoteric school of Paul and Dionysius the Areopagite in Athens, Platonic and Neo-Platonic Christianity was founded. 'Under him [Dionysius] the school had its time of blossoming, because Dionysius taught these mysteries in a wholly special way, while St Paul spread the teaching exoterically.'[17] We cannot describe this school in greater detail now, and only note that our investigations of its mysteries were guided by the fact that 'when we study the Eleusinian Mysteries (that were extirpated root and branch), it is evident that in the first centuries after the Mystery of Golgotha the Risen Christ was Himself present in the Mysteries in order to reform them', a process experienced with great intensity in the present etheric second Mystery of Golgotha.[18]

To understand better the transformation of old anthroposophy through the new Christ impulse, we must contemplate this birth

---

[17] Esoteric lesson of 7 March 1907 (GA 264). See also, Wolfgang Muller, *Dionysius Areopagites* (Verlag die Pforte, Basel 1976).

[18] Lecture of 24 April 1917 (GA 175). A similar process is taking place today, as the etherically Risen Christ is present in the new Michaelic Mysteries, inaugurated by Rudolf Steiner in 1923-4, to inspire us how to reform them, as he reformed the ancient mysteries. The possibility to resurrect old anthroposophy in the twenty-first century is the result of this continued spiritual reformation and transformation.

moment of Dionysian-Pauline Christian Platonism, through the Pauline Damascus Christ event, because it is resurrected today in the knowledge drama of the Second Coming.

In the lecture cycle on *The Philosophy of Thomas Aquinas*, Rudolf Steiner described the Dionysian-Pauline birth of the new, Michael-ic-Christian yoga. As we saw above, it was inspired by the direct perception of the etheric Christ, as He appeared to Paul through His light-giving aura of the Nathanic-Krishna Jesus. And this new Michaelic-Christian yoga was created and practiced by Dionysius in his esoteric school in Athens:

> Dionysius is described as having two paths to the Divine, and so indeed he had ... How can one deal with a personality who gives not one theology, but two: one positive and one negative, one rationalistic and one mystical? For Dionysius, the Divinity was a Being who had to be approached by a rational path, by the finding and giving of names. But he saw that to travel by this path only is to lose the way ... Therefore, in conjunction with it, another way must also be taken, namely, the way that strives towards 'The Nameless'. If a man takes either path alone, he will never find the Divine, but if he takes both paths, then he will find the way to the Divine *at that point at which the two paths cross*... when the human soul finds itself *at their crossing-point*, then both roads together lead to the desired goal. [19]

This is the inversion point of breathing in which everything turns around and inside out: 'at that point in which the two paths cross', the soul finds the way to the divine, that is, to the etheric Christ, when it 'finds itself at their crossing point'. In the modern resurrection of this Dionysian mystery, three mysteries converge and are renewed by the Christ impulse: the ancient mysteries of Eleusis, in which the younger Dionysius appeared and taught in his etheric form; the Platonic academy in Athens, in which Dionysius reincarnated as Plato, who worked with his teacher Socrates to create pure thinking out of the ancient Dionysian initiation in the mysteries[20]; and the first school of esoteric Christianity, described above, inaugurated by the disciple of Paul, Dionysius the Areopagite.

---

[19] Lecture of 23 May 1920 (GA 74). My italics. And see also the lecture of 27 August (GA 129).
[20] Lecture of 24 August 1911 (GA 129).

He was directly guided in the new yoga by the Nathanic-Krishna Jesus to unite the spiritual essence of Platonism, Aristotelism, and Neo-Platonism, with the Pauline experience of the etheric Christ.

The new Krishna, the Nathanic Jesus, brought about the resurrection of his ancient teaching of yoga, and transformed it—in the school of Paul and Dionysius in Athens—into the new path of esoteric Christianity. In his ancient teaching, he disclosed this esoteric secret of breathing. 'Offering inhaling breath into the outgoing breath, and offering the outgoing breath into the inhaling breath, the yogi neutralizes both these breaths; he thus releases the life force from the heart and brings it under his control.'[21] Krishna taught that the archetypal essence exchange of man and the cosmos takes place through breathing. As cosmic sun being, the Christ, incarnated in the being of Krishna, actualized the essence exchange of man and God in the Mystery of Golgotha, when He individualized the divine being and spiritualized the human being. He incarnated the divine Word and spiritualized the human flesh.

The spiritualization of breathing found its first philosophical expression in the dialectical method of Plato and developed further in the Neo-Platonic philosophy of Proclus in the fifth century. In Fichte, Schelling, and Hegel, it found an abstract modern expression, and Herbert Witzenmann applied it to *The Philosophy of Freedom*.[22] For example, it is not difficult to realize that the dialectical movement of thinking in Hegel is a transformed exercise of yoga breathing. In the first stage of his *Logic*, Hegel posits 'being' as thesis and 'nothing' as antithesis, just as inhalation and exhalation stand over against each other. When the 'being', inhalation, and 'nothing', exhalation, are combined, sublimated, and transform each other, 'becoming' is produced.

In the sense of the *Gita* cited above, this is a transformed process of 'offering inhaling breath into the outgoing breath, and offering the outgoing breath into the inhaling breath, and the yogi neutralizes both these breaths'. This releases the pure force of the spirit, the 'soul of dialectic' as Hegel called it, or in the words of the *Gita*, it releases 'the life force from the heart and brings it under his control'.

---

[21] *Bhagavad Gita,* IV:29.

[22] Herbert Witzenmann applied it to *The Philosophy of Freedom* in his book, *Intuition und Beobachtung*, 2nd Teil (Verlag Freies Geistesleben, 1978).

In the Michaelic Yoga described below, this essence exchange takes place between the inhalation of sense-perception and the exhalation of pure thinking, and their synthesis. But for Plato, thinking was not yet a mere abstract shadow of the divine breathing rhythms of the cosmos. He could still experience that when thinking comes to life in the human soul, it is a gift of the gods to human beings, and he experienced the first spark of the cosmic intelligence of Michael as a real spiritual revelation.

This experience finds a clear expression in Plato's dialogue *Philebus*, in which he lets Socrates introduce the 'divine method' as 'a gift from the gods to men... for which there neither is nor ever will be a better way'. It is the supreme art that may have been 'tossed down from some divine source through the agency of a Prometheus together with a gleaming fire, and the ancients, who were better than we and lived nearer the gods', could use them for acquiring the purest knowledge of unchanging ideal archetypes, rather than changing human opinions. In the *Timaeus*, Plato describes how the Demiurge created this 'royal soul and royal reason', along with the other gods, and the 'divine method' is described as the archetype of all divine creation, on a cosmic scale from the highest spiritual perspective.[23]

It was in Paul's esoteric school in Athens, that the first seeds of human thinking, born on earth through Plato and Aristotle, were connected to the Christ impulse for the first time, and continued to inspire and spiritualize thinking up to the late Middle Ages and, indeed, right into the dawn of the age of the Consciousness Soul, as the life and writings of Nicolaus Cusanus show. He could find, in John Scotus Erigena's Latin translations of Dionysius, the spiritual support he needed to consolidate and ground the experience of illumination which he had on the sea coming back from Constantinople to Venice (1437). His *De Docta Ignorantia* (1440) was based on the writings of 'the pupil of St Paul', as he used to refer to Dionysius.[24]

---

[23] Plato's dialogues, like all ancient philosophical texts, have been totally exhausted by the dead modern intellect. But if they are taken up by spiritual scientific practice, enlivened in intensive meditation, they come to life on a higher level, and reveal their great future potentials.

[24] E. Meffert, *Nikolaus von Kues* (Verlag Freies Geistesleben, 1982).

As Rudolf Steiner showed in his lectures on Aquinas[25] and in the karma lectures in 1924, both major streams of thought in the West, in their highest medieval expression in the Platonic-Christian teachings of John of Salisbury, Bernard of Chartres, Bernardus Sylvestris and Alanus ab Insulis, who taught in the school of Chartres in the twelfth century, and in the Aristotelian-Christian Scholasticism of Albertus Magnus and Thomas Aquinas, in the thirteenth century, were still deeply enlivened and animated by the spiritual forces of esoteric Christianity that started in the Pauline stream of Dionysius. For example, in the karma lectures Rudolf Steiner says that when the Platonic teachers from Chartres returned to the spiritual world at the end of the twelfth century, 'the principle of the Mysteries had ascended to the heavens and sent down its Sun-rays thence upon all that was working on the earth [in the Aristotelian stream]'.[26]

In Chartres the esoteric experience and method, formed by Paul and Dionysius directly out to the first etheric Christ event, lit up again and spiritualized thinking through its union with Platonism and Aristotelism. It kept the last vestiges of the original etheric Christ experience alive on the earth until the fifteenth century. Then it all came alive again in its cosmic spiritual form in the supersensible School of Michael in the sun sphere, to prepare the coming of the Aristotelian stream of anthroposophy to the earth in the new Age of Michael. As this preparation in the Michaelic School in the sun sphere was reaching its culmination, at the end of the eighteenth century and the beginning of the nineteenth century, a mighty earthly inspiration and reflection took place on the earth. There, during the shortest and most condensed time span, an unprecedented assembly of some of the greatest teachers of humanity took place. We cannot explore this in greater detail here and will only point out the fact that in this short century, from 1750 to 1850, through the power of the newly reincarnating German Folk Spirit, the leaders and Prophets of the Hebrew people (whose Folk Spirit at that time was Michael) reincarnated in Germany, after they had assimilated the Greek spirit and Platonic and Aristotelian thinking in their intermediate Greek and Roman

---

[25] GA 74, 1920.
[26] Lecture of 14 July 1924 (GA 237).

incarnations.[27] This took place on earth, while in the sun sphere above, Michael led his pupils to the powerful 'cosmic cultus', summarizing the previous centuries of cosmic teaching and preparing the coming of the Aristotelian part of anthroposophy to the earth at the beginning of the twentieth century.

There, on the earth, we could see a first reflection of this Michaelic School, in German Idealism and Romanticism, though it was still clothed in the garments of older times. Therefore, we cannot find it in the intellectual forms of the dialectical thinking of Fichte, Schelling and Hegel, but in the inner energy and inspiration behind them; it could light up only partially, for example, through Lessing's last book, *The Education of the Human Race*, Schiller's experience of creative freedom in the *Letters on the Aesthetic Education of Man*, and it became almost spiritually tangible in Goethe's living conception of metamorphosis and his fairy tale of *The Green Snake and Beautiful Lily*. It was also still alive in Novalis' spiritualized magical idealism and Schelling's late philosophy. This supersensible Michaelic inspiration was shared in the philosophical, scientific, and artistic creations of so many creative people in this unprecedented gathering of creative human spirits on the earth, because in this short creative century Michael was working most intimately with the incarnating German Folk Spirit, striving to lay the foundations for his coming age.

And then, when the German Folk Spirit ascended back to the spiritual world, it was the task of Rudolf Steiner, working in all loneliness—in real freedom—in the most materialistic time in human evolution, to inaugurate the School of Michael on the earth at the beginning of the twentieth century, preparing its possible culmination and transition from the twentieth to the twenty-first century.

In his time Plato conceived the divine, dialectical art of thinking out of the last extracts of inspiration and respiration from the ancient mysteries and Oriental yoga. He could experience the last rays of the cosmic light of wisdom, streaming from cosmic Sophia, and transformed them into Philo-Sophia. In passing it on to his pupil, Aristotle, he told him, 'I will withdraw myself for a time...

---

[27] This group was led by Goethe and Novalis, the German reincarnations of Moses and Elijah. Some of their Hebrew initiations are described in my book, *Jerusalem: The Role of the Hebrew People in the Spiritual Biography of Humanity* (Temple Lodge 2019).

and will leave you to yourself. In the world of thought, for which you are so especially endowed, and which will become the thought-world of humanity for many centuries, try to build up in thoughts what you have learned here in my school.' So Plato and Aristotle separated, and Plato therewith fulfilled, as commanded, a high spiritual mission through Aristotle.[28] And as we shall show below, one of the main tasks of the true anthroposophical Platonism at the end of the last century was to spiritualize the old anthroposophical Aristotelism, synthesize both in their new form, and resurrect the Platonic 'divine method'. But both streams could only be spiritualized through the meeting with the etheric Christ, because only this source of wholly new spiritual forces could bring both to Imaginative consciousness. Building on this foundation, one could use this united spiritual force to create the knowledge drama of the Second Coming and build the foundations for the new School of Michael in the twenty-first century.[29]

As Aristotle had to kill the divine method of Plato, and transform it into earthly logical thinking, Rudolf Steiner's karmic task was to resurrect this dead dialectic and create modern spiritual science out of it. In the way he grasps the living essence of Dialectic, we can find the seed of its resurrection through the etheric Christ impulse and the Michaelic Yoga. 'Dialectic is the life of logic, and whoever understands the spirit of dialectic, touches the higher realms of cognition, and transforms the rigid, dead concepts into living ones, that is, distributes them among certain people. He turns logic into a conversation. Hence Plato's dialectical logic turned it into a conversation. "What is more noble than Gold?" inquired the King. "Light," replied the Snake. "What is more beautiful than the light?" asked the King. "The conversation"!'[30] This millennia-long conversation and essence exchange between Plato and Aristotle, underlined the entire evolution of human thinking in the last 2500 years. And it reached another fruitful meeting and culmination in the Platonic-Aristotelian essence exchange at the end of the last century, described below.

---

[28] Lecture of 14 December 1923 (GA 232).

[29] This process is described in detail in my book, *The Twilight and Resurrection of Humanity: The History of the Michaelic Movement since the Death of Rudolf Steiner. An Esoteric Study* (Temple Lodge, 2020).

[30] Lecture of 7 July 1904 (GA 89).

It must be emphasized that the anthroposophical Platonic-Aristotelian essence exchange since the end of last century, is possible only due to the present Damascus experience. The meeting with the etheric Christ alone offers the new spiritual forces, that make the resurrection of anthroposophy possible. In this respect too, the Pauline Christ experience from 2000 years ago is the archetype of the modern Christ experience.

Paul was equally schooled in esoteric Jewish lore and Greek philosophy. Confronting the Jews, he experienced the same violent rejection that Jesus experienced shortly before him, from 'the Pharisees and doctors of the law'. About them Jesus said that they 'hold the keys to the kingdom of heaven, but don't use them to enter the spiritual worlds, nor let anybody else enter'. The same was Paul's experience with the learned Greek philosophers in Athens. When he came to Athens, he addressed the Greek philosophers in the Areopagus sermon, described by his pupil, Luke. He began it by the historically significant words:

> As I walked around and looked carefully at your objects of worship, I even found an altar with this inscription: TO AN UNKNOWN GOD. So you are ignorant of the very thing you worship—and this is what I am going to proclaim to you.[31]

When we speak about the present Christ experience to the learned 'Pharisees and doctors of spiritual science', we find ourselves in the same situation of Paul, when he spoke to the Pharisees in Jerusalem and the philosophers in Athens. A century ago, modern spiritual science was given to humanity to prepare the Second Coming, as in the time of Christ's first coming Jerusalem and Athens prepared the first coming. And yet, when we speak 2000 years after Paul about the modern Damascus event, a whole century after the death of Rudolf Steiner, we find very little understanding, not to mention fierce opposition. We realize that the living Christ is as unknown today as He was to the people of ancient Greek and Judea in the time of Jesus and Paul. For this reason, I placed the post-mortem words of the Chief of the German General Staff, Helmuth von Moltke, as the motto to my book, *The Spiritual Event of the 20th Century: the occult*

---

[31] Acts 17:16–34.

significance of the 12 years 1933-1945 in the light of spiritual science, published in 1993:

> There we are already [at the end of the twentieth century] after 'the appearance of the Sun' that has to take place in etheric Imagination for earthly life. The Christ will appear for the Earth when almost everyone has abandoned Him; when all that mankind knows of Him is His name.[32]

The New Experience of the Supersensible was published in 1995 to describe, as comprehensively as I could at that time, 'the appearance of the Sun', *that had indeed taken place in etheric Imagination*, and was and still is largely ignored. In preparing the 2nd edition after some 30 years, I do so with the hope that in the third decade of the twenty-first century it will find some free and courageous human hearts to read and experience the Michaelic signs of the time.

---

[32] The Message from Helmuth von Moltke was transmitted to his wife, Eliza von Moltke, through Rudolf Steiner, in: *Helmuth von Moltke 1848-1916, Dokumente zu seinem Wirken*. (Letter 74, 27 March 1919, Perseus Verlag, Basel 1993.)

Chapter 2
The Michaelic Yoga

'We must develop this new Yoga will'

As we mentioned above, Rudolf Steiner pointed out often that the Damascus event of Paul was the first experience of its kind, preparing what will begin for humanity in 1933. But the modern Damascus event is taking place on the level of the Consciousness Soul, and it has as its foundation of knowledge not the ancient mystery knowledge that Plato, Aristotle, Paul and Dionysius still possessed, but modern spiritual science.

It is deeply grounded in Rudolf Steiner's karma and in the karma of the Michaelic School, that its real future mission could only begin in the last years and months of his previous life.[33] This means that he could only gradually connect the spiritual stream of Michael with the anthroposophical movement, and when this could begin in 1924, it was so short-lived on the earth. His own spiritual path was always based on the spiritual activity of *The Philosophy of Freedom*, coupled with the creative forces of Goethe. But he had to wait 25 years to publish the 2nd edition of *The Philosophy of Freedom* in 1918, because his pupils showed no interest in this 'non-anthroposophical' book. But, as a matter of fact, *The Philosophy of Freedom* is a non-*theosophical* book and the pre-eminent foundation of all anthroposophical spiritual science. Indeed, it is his most anthroposophical book. If we take seriously into account what Rudolf Steiner said about its significance, *The Philosophy of Freedom* is the eternally living and creative seed and source of future anthroposophy. This can be understood if we truly experience what Rudolf Steiner meant in his answer to Walter Johannes Stein's question. Stein asked, 'What will remain from your work after thousands of years?' To which he replied, 'Only *The Philosophy of Freedom*. But in this

---

[33] This mystery of the karma of Rudolf Steiner and the Age of Michael, in the last and present century, is described in greater detail in the *Twilight and Resurrection of Humanity*.

book, everything is contained. If one actualizes the activity of freedom [Freiheits*akt*] described there, one will find the whole content of Anthroposophy.'[34]

This makes the publishing of the 2nd edition of *The Philosophy of Freedom* in 1918, seven years before his death, into an event of a fresh new beginning. And this explains why only during 1919-1920 could he also present the new Michaelic Yoga practice. This deed became at the end of the twentieth century a decisive one, because then *The Philosophy of Freedom* could become what it was destined to become: the foundation of the Michaelic Yoga and the way to connect the resurrected anthroposophy with the etheric Christ through the modern Pauline experience. This turning point, which was described in detail also in my book, *Cognitive Yoga: Making Yourself a New Etheric Body and Individuality*, became the most natural and timely foundation of the knowledge drama of the Second Coming.

The Michaelic Yoga practice, called by Rudolf Steiner 'the new will of Yoga', was described for the first time in the 1919 lecture cycle about the mission of Michael, exactly 40 years after the beginning of the new Michael Age.[35] A year later it was transformed into a new path of spiritual-scientific development, in the first lecture cycle of the School of Spiritual Science in the almost completed first Goetheanum. This was a momentous event for the future evolution of anthroposophy, because for the first time Rudolf Steiner could merge into one spiritual practice his earliest work with Goethe and *The Philosophy of Freedom* and transform it into a new spiritua-scientific practice.

Let us bring before us some of Rudolf Steiner's original words not to merely 'understand' the concepts, or feel the related subjective emotions, but experience in our *active heart and will* forces their living spiritual breathing and heartbeat, because in these rhythms Michael's heart is pulsing today in the etheric world, with which our etheric hearts must be united.

---

[34] W. J. Stein / Rudolf Steiner: *Dokumentation eines wegweisenden Zusammenwirkens*, Verlag am Goetheanum, 1985. This is the reason why *The Philosophy of Freedom* could become the source and foundation of the knowledge drama of the Second Coming.

[35] Lecture of 30 November 1919 (GA 194).

In the lecture from 30 November, 1919, about the mission of Michael, Rudolf Steiner described this process in this way:

> When our sense processes will become ensouled again, we shall have established a crossing point, and in this crossing point we shall take hold of the human will that streams up... Then we shall, at the same time, have the subjective-objective element for which Goethe was longing so very much. We shall have the possibility of grasping, in a sensitive way, the peculiar nature of the sense process of man in its relation to the outer world... In reality, there takes place a soul process from the outside toward the inside, which is taken hold of by the deeply subconscious, inner soul process, so that the two processes overlap. From outside, cosmic thoughts work into us, from inside, humanity's will works outward. Humanity's will and cosmic thought cross in this crossing point, just as the objective and the subjective element once crossed in the breath. We must learn to feel how our will works through our eyes and how the activity of the senses delicately mingles with it, bringing about the crossing of cosmic thoughts and humanity's will. *We must develop this new Yoga will...* This must be the endeavour of the fifth post-Atlantean period; namely, the endeavour to find something in the human inner life in which an outer process takes place at the same time.[36]

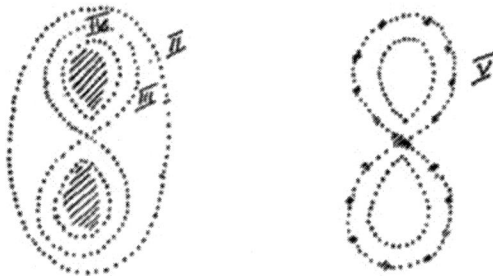

A year later, in the lecture cycle on the *Boundaries of Natural Science*, we find the following description of the new Michaelic Yoga method:

> Pure thinking is related to exhalation just as perception is related to inhalation... by bringing movement into the life of

---

[36] 'The Ancient Yoga Culture and the New Yoga Will. The Michael Culture of the Future', lecture from 30 November 1919 (GA 194).

the soul, one experiences the pendulum, the rhythm, the continual interpenetrating vibration of perception and thinking... the Westerner achieves a kind of breathing of the soul-spirit in place of the physical breathing of the yogi ... And gradually, by means of this rhythmic pulse, by means of this rhythmic breathing process in perception and thinking, he struggles to rise up to spiritual reality in Imagination, Inspiration and Intuition... The Oriental says: systole, diastole; inhalation, exhalation. In place of these the Westerner must put perception and thinking. Where the Oriental speaks of the development of physical breathing, we in the West say development of a breathing of the soul-spirit within the cognitional process through perception and thinking.[37]

The Oriental pupil of yoga was led through his breathing exercises to experience his immortal spiritual being beyond birth and death. In our time, when this higher being of humanity, the etheric Christ, appears again in our etheric midst, clothed in His etheric garment and radiating with spiritual light through the Nathanic-Krishna being, we experience how He lives, moves and becomes with us. He breathes etherically with us, walks among us, befriends us, when we search for His spirit friendship and council. He then becomes our soul—and spirit companion, a fountain of eternal life—and light-giving etheric breathing. In the past, the spiritual being that dwelt in the physical air, was experienced by the yoga pupils:

What does the Eastern student of yoga attain by surrendering himself to conscious, regulated, varied breathing? Oh, he experiences something quite extraordinary when he inhales. When inhaling he experiences a quality of air that is not found when we experience air as a purely physical substance but only when we unite ourselves with the air and thus comprehend it spiritually. As he breathes in, a genuine

---

[37] Lecture of 3 October 1920 (GA 322). The same method was described again—from a somewhat different aspect—as the anthroposophical method that can make of the Anthroposophical Society a preliminary school of true modern initiation, in the spirit of the Christmas Foundation Meeting. (*Leading Thoughts*, 'Understanding of the Spirit; Conscious Experience of Destiny', 13 July 1924, GA 26.)

student of yoga experiences something that works forma-
tively upon his whole being, that works spiritually; something that does not expend itself in the life between birth
and death, but, entering into us through the spirituality of
the outer air, engenders in us something that passes with
us through the portal of death. To experience the breathing process consciously means taking part in something
that persists when we have laid aside the physical body...
To grasp the breathing process consciously means to comprehend ourselves beyond birth and death.[38]

The present Michaelic task of the modern spiritual scientist is,
therefore, to learn how to etherize and spiritualize his thinking
and sense perceptions. He does so if he learns to separate thinking
from sense perception and stops the instinctive process of forming
representations. As we show in *Cognitive Yoga*, we 'electrolyze' the
hard 'water' of our mental images and representations, separate
and liberate the pure 'gases' (etheric forces) of sense-perception
from pure thinking from their bondage to the brain-bound intellect. Then we can exhale this etherized thinking outside our body
and inhale the etherized sense perceptions into our etheric body.
When he accomplishes this, pure etherized thinking and etherized
sense perceptions are transformed into Imagination and Inspiration. And when we succeed in crossing them together, then at their
crossing point, we achieve the faculty of Intuition:

An essential prerequisite is, as I have said, to have thought
through *The Philosophy of Freedom* beforehand. This is then
left, so to speak, to one side, while pursuing the inner path
of contemplation, of meditation [on the other side]. What can
be experienced in *The Philosophy of Freedom* as pure thinking
has, as a result of our having worked inwardly on our souls in
another sphere [of pure sense perception], become something
utterly different. It has become fuller, richer in content. While
on the one hand we have penetrated into our inner being and
have deepened our power of Imagination, on the other hand
we have raised what resulted from our mental work on *The
Philosophy of Freedom*, up out of ordinary consciousness.
Thoughts that formerly had floated more or less abstractly

---

[38] Lecture of 3 October 1920 (GA 322).

within pure thinking have been transformed into substantial forces that are alive in our consciousness: what once was pure thought is now Inspiration. We have developed Imagination, and pure thinking has become Inspiration. Following this path further, we become able to keep apart what we have gained following two paths that must be sharply differentiated... Now we can bring these modes of experience together. We can unite the inner with the outer. The fusion of Imagination and Inspiration brings us in turn to *Intuition*.[39]

When this method is added to the occult training methods and meditations offered in the books *Knowledge of the Higher Worlds* and *Occult Science,* it complements them in the most fruitful manner, by the direct spiritualization of the main forces of the Consciousness Soul: free thinking and sense-perception, as Goethe and Rudolf Steiner practiced them. As Rudolf Steiner emphasized in these lectures, this path can make us into fully active and creative contemporaries in the modern scientific and social world. Through the transformation of sense-perception, this method can bring about a resurrection of Goetheanism in anthroposophy. And when the resurrection of Goetheanism is crossed with the result of the transformation of thinking according to *The Philosophy of Freedom,* etherized thinking and sense-perception mutually fertilize each other. Then man is enabled 'to understand through the *earthly* forces the coming Christ impulse; this is the connection between the world of thoughts in *The Philosophy* of *Freedom* and the higher forces of knowledge that evolve in our soul'.[40]

Modern spiritual science reached maturity in this moment, because a direct and continued line of development was established, that leads—without any interruption—from Rudolf Steiner's fundamental scientific and philosophical works to the most mature anthroposophical achievements in the last years of his life. Only by means of this practice can we find the truly modern way to the most important event in the evolution of humanity and the earth in our age: the new appearance of the Christ in the etheric world. Only in this way can we illuminate His etheric appearance with the resurrected light of Michael's intelligence and thinking.

---

[39] Lecture of 3 October 1920 (GA 322).
[40] Lecture of 5 March 1914 (GA 152).

This practice underlies the spiritual research presented in Chapter 5 of *The New Experience of the Supersensible*, called the knowledge drama of the Second Coming, the aim of which is to individualize independently the given meeting with the Christ and lead to the second meeting, through the development of Michael's new will of yoga. The mutual fertilization and spiritualization between the outbreathing of etherized thinking and the inbreathing of etheric perception, brings about 'the connection between the world of thoughts in *The Philosophy* of *Freedom* and the higher forces of knowledge', by means of which the appearance of the etheric Christ in the etheric world can be scientifically investigated.

Chapter 3
The Platonic-Aristotelian Essence Exchange at the End of the Twentieth Century

The basic structure of *The New Experience of the Supersensible* is an expression of the two pillars of the modern Christ experience: the *given* meeting with the etheric Christ and the *consciously gained* meeting. The given meeting is described in Chapter 4 and the consciously gained meeting in Chapter 5. The book is based, therefore, on the relation between the given and consciously gained Christ experience. Philosophically speaking, the two meetings can be compared to the cognitive connection established between the 'given percept' and the 'actively produced concept'. We perceive the things around us with our senses all the time. But how many times do we stop to think and inquire about their nature, being and becoming? Most often we simply move on, being occupied by other things.

More pictorially, we can use the language of the Grail story. Its basic cognitive formation is the same. It describes the path that leads from the merely given impression, experienced by Parsifal in his 'first visit' to the Grail Castle. He just looked at the Grail procession and the anguish of the Fisher King—but did not inquire about them. He did not ask any question about what he observed. He remained a passive 'onlooker' and the experience of the Grail mysteries remained a 'given percept'. Parsifal did not think and inquire about its causes, and therefore did not ask any question. Only after much suffering and doubts, did he realize his omission, and then he could search consciously for the way back to the castle, that led him through 'sixty miles' of probations. And in the second visit he understood what he merely looked at in the first visit. He added to the given 'percept' the actively formed 'concept', realized the truth of the situation, and acted accordingly.

Another imagination that was often found fruitful, is based on Goethe's fairy tale *The Green Snake and the Beautiful Lily*, where he describes the construction of the bridge that connects the given spiritual experience with the consciously accomplished spiritual research.

The bridge was defined by Rudolf Steiner in this way:

> Spiritual Science works from below upwards, stretches out its
> hands as it were from below upwards to grasp the hands of

Michael stretching down from above. *It is then that the bridge can be created between man and the Gods.* [41]

This bridge is built from the given Christ experience, the supersensible 'percept', across to the fully conscious spiritual-scientific research, that produces the 'concept' for this 'percept'. In this case, the 'percept' is the appearance, words, and deeds of the etheric Christ, experienced in the first meeting, and the 'concept' is the second meeting, gained in the conscious spiritual research of the knowledge drama of the Second Coming. The supersensible 'percept' is described in Chapter 4, entitled, 'The Modern Christ Experience—The Meeting with the New Initiator'. The spiritual-scientific creation process of the related 'concept' of this experience is described in Chapter 6, 'The Knowledge Drama of the Second Coming'.

In the philosophical tradition, the 'concept' belongs to the Platonic side, and the 'percept' to the Aristotelian, and the riddles of the synthesis of percept and concept have occupied philosophers over the last 2500 years. Rudolf Steiner planted the seed of the Platonic-Aristotelian 'essence exchange' in *The Philosophy of Freedom* in 1894 and transformed it into the Michaelic Yoga in the lectures on the *Boundaries of Natural Science* in 1920. It proved a most fruitful foundation of the knowledge drama of the Second Coming and the construction of Goethe's bridge that leads from the given to the consciously gained meeting with the etheric Christ.

In this chapter, we will describe the formation process of the Platonic-Aristotelian essence exchange, developed in the 1980s and 1990s. While I am writing this short Prelude to the new edition of *The New Experience of the Supersensible* after three decades, I find it necessary to also describe some aspects of my personal path, because in the search for the Grail, the universal and personal are intimately intertwined.

My adult spiritual life began with the above-mentioned experience of the supersensible 'percept'. But at this age, I did not yet have the spiritual knowledge to create the necessary 'concept' to grasp and understand it. The given meeting with the etheric Christ, described below, was a pure supersensible percept, experienced without any concept to explain it. And therefore, my search for the consciously formed 'concept' was from the beginning fully conscious spiritual research, because a supersensible 'percept' can only be matched by an equally living and spiritual 'concept'. In other

---

[41] Lecture of 17 December 1922 (GA 219). My italics.

words, I understood early on that I would have to create my individual path on the go, and the knowledge that I gained would have to be as living as the given Christ experience.

When one starts from conscious supersensible experience, one is not confronted with an abstract problem of knowledge, but with an existential problem of life, of having to live, perceive and think in two opposite worlds and dimensions. On the one hand, I was struggling to transform the supersensible experience into concepts and words, by means of which I could represent it in ordinary consciousness. I had to work spiritually from above downward, from the supersensible 'percept', which was given as a spiritual gift of grace, towards my ordinary daily cognition. But my daily cognition could not grasp it by means of my earthly forces. I had to find ways to empower and spiritualize it and lead it to meet the supersensible halfway or in the middle. For this purpose, I had to use the given life forces from the supersensible experience, to gradually spiritualize the 'concept' formation of earthly cognition, to lift it to the etheric world, and apply it to the Christ experience. And in this manner, the first part of my life, that continued until the middle of my 30s, was dedicated to this constant effort, to 'bridge' the two worlds in which I lived. I was striving to create the spiritual path to connect the supersensible 'percept' with the equivalent spiritualized 'concept'.

My spiritual activity became a life-giving soul breathing, inhaling my spiritual experiences and exhaling my conscious spiritual activity, repeatedly incarnating and excarnating, connecting the two worlds, without which I could not feel myself to be a whole human being, nor achieve reliable knowledge of these experiences. And in the first year after the Christ experience, the intensive study of Rudolf Steiner's books and lectures was the only real bridging experience, that allowed me to breathe spiritually and achieve this initial existential and cognitive wholeness. Each word and sentence was experienced as life-giving breaths, connecting the given and actively gained supersensible life and knowledge. But this breathing was confined to the actual time of study and meditation, while in ordinary life I was unable to kindle this light by means of my free spiritual activity.

This situation changed when I read *The Philosophy of Freedom* for the first time in Easter 1976, exactly a year after the given Christ experience. I realized, even in the first reading, that I could produce in my thinking the same spiritual light that was given as gift in the Christ experience. I experienced immediately—though of course it took many years to actualize this in practical detail—that the spiritual light given in the Christ experience and the light of pure thinking, originate from the same spiritual source. I was immensely relieved because I could begin to breathe spiritually, inhale and exhale between the spiritual and physical worlds, as a free being. I found a free and active force in my soul, which I could activate at any time, through which I could connect the two sides of my existence. I remember most vividly what I experienced laying down *The Philosophy of Freedom* after the first reading. I said to myself: Now you can breathe freely between the two sides of your life and cognition, whenever you wish to activate this truly magical gift of pure thinking. Therefore, I immediately started to build the bridge between the worlds, letting pure thinking and etheric perception enhance each other. And this experience led me, in the first years of my 20s, to form the idea and ideal of the 'bridge', in its initial form.

To understand the biography of the bridge construction and the Platonic-Aristotelian essence exchange that underlies it, it is important to note that when the Sentient Soul develops at the age of 21-28, it is largely embedded in the soul world. This means that the physical experiences of the senses and the thinking connected with the senses, is veiled by astral and etheric veils. During the seven years, 28-35, the Mind Soul develops in the etheric world, and man draws nearer to the physical world but experiences it still only through etheric perception. Only with the development of the Consciousness Soul between 35-42, can man enter for the first time fully into the modern experience of the physical senses and consciousness. The Consciousness Soul is the new soul member, that began its development in the fifteenth century, and this means that we did not experience nor develop it in previous incarnations. Therefore, its spiritual development is the new task of modern spiritual science. That part of the Platonic-Aristotelian essence exchange, described below, took place in the 14 years between 21 and 35, in the development of the Sentient and Mind Souls, that prepared the spiritualization of the Consciousness Soul after the middle of life.[42]

---

[42] In terms of the bridge construction, this means that until the middle of life, mainly the first, etheric-cognitive layer was formed, from head to heart. This part could therefore be reported more fully in the 1st edition of *The New Experience of the Supersensible*. The construction of the second and third layers of the bridge, from heart to limbs, is described in greater detail in the new edition of the book.

Towards the end of my 20s I came to the point in which I could say to myself: Regarding the development of pure thinking, based on *Goethe's World Conception, Truth and Science, The Philosophy of Freedom* and *Riddles of Philosophy*, I have made some progress. I noticed that it caused two related changes in my thinking and imaginative faculties. Thinking became more akin to Imagination, and the given Imaginative faculties were transformed by thinking. On the one hand, I could penetrate and enhance my Imaginative perception and imbue it with the clear light of pure thinking. This enabled me to unite the actively produced 'concept' and given supersensible 'percept' in greater clarity. On the other hand, the forces of Imaginative perception spiritualized the thinking and lifted it to the level of Imagination. Spiritualized thinking gave consistency and clarity to Imaginative perception, Imaginative perception transformed spiritualized thinking to Imaginative perception. As I reached the end of my 20s, I could feel this as a significant progress. The essence exchange between spiritualized thinking and Imagination became one stream, with two closely related functions, and I could use it as a mature and robust cognitive capacity, to build the first stable and secure part of the bridge.

In the essence exchange between thought-through imagination and Imaginative thinking I felt myself in my spiritual home. I felt that in this activity, 'the Platonic spirit which had been living for a long time in the development of Christianity... found its true development... for Platonism is absorbed by human beings ever and again. Again and again at one place or another it becomes *the staff by which men draw themselves upward*. And Platonism, as we know, entered most significantly into all that was taught in the School of Chartres'.[43] In this free spiritual activity, I could truly experience how 'the staff by which men draw themselves upward' came to life in my soul, whenever I imbued the given Christ experience with the pure thinking of *The Philosophy of Freedom* and spiritualized this thinking with the supersensible life forces of the etheric Christ.

---

[43] Lecture of 23 September 1924 (GA 238). My italics. The platonic 'spiritual staff' of pure thinking was created before thinking has descended to the physical brain. It used foremost the etheric brain, and therefore, as we shall presently see, it could not yet be regarded as an expression of the Consciousness Soul, the soul member fully grounded in the physical body.

Furthermore, now I could stand within the etheric world of the living supersensible 'percept', and from the etheric world 'look down' and grasp the changes caused by this spiritualized thinking in the etheric body. I could perceive the lively engraved footsteps of spiritualized thinking in the higher part of the etheric body, through which the forces of Imaginative perception operate. In this etheric part transformed by spiritualized thinking, my spiritual being and activity in the soul and etheric worlds were reflected, and the Christ experience could be brought to ever clearer Imaginative contours and forms.

The new force of spiritual light, which came from the spiritualized thinking of *The Philosophy of Freedom*, allowed me to perceive much more clearly in this part of the etheric body the reflected results of my Imaginative investigations in the etheric world. It was as if this spiritualized thinking transformed part of the etheric body into an etheric mirror, that could reflect the Imaginative experiences, as the physical brain reflects ordinary sense perceptions and representations. I could in this way begin to 'remember' my etheric-imaginative experiences and investigations in the etheric world and carry them consciously from 'over there' to the *spiritualized part* of my ordinary consciousness 'down here' and identify them as two sides of the same knowledge process; I could, for the first time, achieve a continuation of consciousness from the given etheric perception to the etheric imprints of spiritualized thinking.

These were results of the free spiritual activity that I actualized in pure thinking in the physical world. This side of the bridge extended now from imaginative consciousness to spiritualized thinking; I could also feel that the supersensible self-consciousness, given with the 'I' of Christ, could connect with my ordinary 'I', to the extent that the 'I' was active in spiritualized thinking. The moment of the self-conscious meeting of my two 'I's by means of the bridge of the spiritualized thinking of *The Philosophy of Freedom*, was a great event, described also in the first lecture of *The Twilight and Resurrection of Humanity*. My spiritual existence and life in the etheric world and the free activity of my 'I' in pure thinking became one continuous stream, because the Imaginative perceptions and experiences were reflected in the etheric mirror created by spiritualized thinking in the etheric body. In the etheric body—not yet in the physical—I could experience both sides of my being as belonging to the same 'I'.

The result of the first decade of my spiritual life can therefore be summarized as follows. A new faculty was created, the result of the spiritualization of thinking by means of the Imaginative faculties given as part of the meeting with the etheric Christ. The essence exchange between Imaginative cognition and spiritualized thinking, spiritualized both activities in continuous breathing cycles and rhythms of intensification. It united both in a higher synthesis and created the first side of the bridge of the continuation of consciousness.

However, I knew that the bridge was built from above downward and reached only the upper side of the etheric body. My ordinary cognitive life in the physical world, that runs its course in sense-perceptions and the forming of mental pictures, was below this etheric mirror, and was not directly accessible to my higher forces of cognition. As long as I was busy with completing the first part of the etheric layer of the bridge, I was aware of this situation, but was fully engaged in the etheric formation described above. Once it was completed, however, I could turn my attention to ordinary consciousness in the physical world, that became now much closer to spiritual perception.

I consider the next stage of my life, to which the greater part of my 30s belong, to be the most important in the first part of my life. In the development of the Mind Soul, the bridge construction faced new challenges, because of the new nearness to the physical world. It posed fundamental riddles and challenges of the knowledge drama of the Second Coming. This has to do with the difficult double problem of spiritual memory.

First, how does one carry over an echo of self-consciousness, produced in the physical world, across the Threshold? In the given Imaginative experience, the memory of our 'I' in the physical world is greatly subdued. We do not really know—as long as the experience lasts—that we are the physical self that we know ourselves to be in the physical world. The correlate of this is that when we awaken back in ordinary earthly self-consciousness, we cannot fully grasp and remember our spiritual experiences. But this changes the more the development of the Mind Soul progresses in the 30s, and especially when the approaching Consciousness Soul is felt, after the 33rd year of life.

The reason is that when you begin your adult life with a given spiritual experience and faculties, you realize that ordinary self-consciousness, that we take for granted nowadays, develops only gradually, and becomes mature only in the middle of life. You experience it in its true nature only very gradually. Until the age of 28, the development of the Sentient Soul is still wholly immersed in the supersensible experience. Ordinary consciousness begins to shimmer through during the development of the Mind Soul during 28-35. But only after the age of 33, do you begin to feel the entry of the forces of the Consciousness Soul that make you a real citizen of the physical world. Only after we reach 33 and indeed, in its true significance, not before 35-6, do we experience an unbridgeable abyss between supersensible and physical consciousness. For the first time, we can say that we experience a state of consciousness into which the supersensible experience does not naturally flow.

It is also forgotten much faster than in the previous 14 years. The Consciousness Soul dams the inflow of the supersensible, and a soul life begins, for the first time, that is wholly separated from given spiritual experiences. On the other hand, what we experience in ordinary consciousness, that is based on physical sense impressions and intellectual reflection, is also easily lost when we turn our attention away from it. And of course, in this state, there is no question of being able to spiritualize and carry it to the supersensible experience outside the body.

This is the reason why we lose our ordinary sense-perceptions, thoughts, and self-consciousness when we fall asleep each night. Now we begin to distinguish between the stage of self-consciousness, experienced through the bodily senses, and what we experienced previously in imaginative cognition. In given imaginative perception we are fully conscious, but we still lack the *self*-consciousness that we are now learning to develop and experience on earth. This means that we cannot remember distinctly, during our experiences outside the body, who we are on earth, and conversely, we cannot bring the spiritual experiences into the required sharp focus in physical consciousness. This situation develops only gradually from the 20s to the 30s and becomes an actual problem only after the age of 33.

In other words, until the end of my 20s I could bridge my consciousness from above downward, to the upper layers of the etheric body, where spiritualized thinking united with imaginative perception. Indeed, the etheric mirror created by means of spiritualized thinking, allowed me to some extent to express in pictorial images, a trace and echo of the imaginative experiences. This was a source of great satisfaction, but also, on the other hand, in my 30s it sharpened the experience that my consciousness was still divided, and the forces of spiritual knowledge could not penetrate the physical body and world. There was always a barrier and veil that separated the light of my imaginative perception and cognition from the light of *this* world. I felt that I was not fully incarnated as other people are. And I intensified my search for the cognitive forces, from which such strong forces might come, that would allow me to extend the bridge from the etheric to the physical world.

In my ordinary consciousness, I could very well portray the goal of the bridge work ahead, in its ideal form. And as I approached the middle of my 30s, I knew that a crucial probation concerning the knowledge drama of the Second Coming would begin. I knew what would be required to build the second part of the bridge: the death forces in the physical brain and world would have to be confronted in the Pauline sense: 'And now, when Paul understood this, he realized for the first time the truth of esoteric Christianity. The assimilation of death into life: this is the secret of Golgotha.'[44] Therefore, it was clear to me that to enter with my whole being into earthly consciousness, I had to find the path that leads from the etheric to the physical brain, from the forces of life to the forces of death, from the formative forces of imaginative cognition to the formative forces of physical consciousness. I knew that this must be the key to the riddle of how to individualize the 'I' gift and transform the given Christ meeting into a voluntary meeting. But as I tried to solve this riddle, striving to create the soul forces to overcome the death forces of ordinary consciousness, I encountered great obstacles.

The main difficulty was that the construction of the bridge from the etheric to the physical body requires sacrificing a portion of its natural life forces. This is the opposite process of the spiritualization of thinking, described above. Pure thinking is essentially an etheric process, to which the physical body does not contribute, and the etheric forces used for its spiritualization are vitalized and enhanced in this process. The etheric forces that spiritualize thinking, taken from the Christ experience, are akin to the etheric forces of pure thinking, and mutually enhanced each other in

---

[44] Lecture of 2 April 1922 (GA 211). And see Chapter 1, above.

this process. In other words, the spiritualization of thinking and of Imaginative cognition is essentially a building process, while the incarnation into the physical brain is mainly a process of destruction. The etheric forces that you apply to the physical body, simply to perceive with the physical senses, die in each sense-perception; if you want to incarnate consciously into the nerves-senses system, and fully inhabit your physical brain, you must *consciously* kill in your etheric body living and vibrant forces, that otherwise sustain and enliven not only the growth forces of the physical body, but also the forces of imaginative perception and cognition. And you know that only this self-conscious killing, performed voluntarily in the etheric body, would allow you to fully incarnate into the physical brain. There, in the brain, could be grasped the inherently devitalized formative forces of ordinary sense-perception, thinking and self-consciousness. This seemed to pose an unsolvable riddle, because how could the life forces, if you kill them while entering the physical brain, spiritualize the forces that kill them?

After all the theoretical answers to this riddle were considered, I knew that I had to begin to do it, to find out what happens in practice, as in any other field of spiritual research. The major difference however, had to be dealt with first, namely, that previously I experienced the intensification of the upbuilding etheric forces, with which the human soul feels itself naturally allied, and now, I had to connect myself willingly with the forces of destruction and take them into my heart.

And the human soul experiences the upbuilding and destructive forces differently because it feels naturally that its essence is allied with the upbuilding forces, and it has a strong inclination to avoid the forces of death and destruction. It must be emphasized, therefore, that one can change this original disposition of the soul, only because of the given meeting with the etheric Christ, described in Chapter 4 of *The New Experience of the Supersensible*. Man can only 'assimilate death into life' to the extent that one experiences that 'not "I" but the "I" of Christ', is taking the forces of death into Himself.

As I entered my 30s this became increasingly an existential situation. On the spiritual side, imaginative cognition was experienced as a life-giving stream, because it connected me to the universal source of life, but on the earthly side life was full of riddles and obstacles. And then at one specific turn along this path—I had just turned 30 at that time—the following occurred. At this stage, I had already covered some anthroposophical ground and indeed I was, in certain respects, after many wanderings, already 'in sight' of the solution to this destiny and spirit riddle, to whose solution I dedicated the first part of my spiritual life; I was, nevertheless, in relation to the above-described central riddles of incarnation and death still 'in the dark wood of 60 miles'. To understand this situation some spiritual-scientific explanation is due, to place this 'turning point in the middle of the path' between the 'first given visit' and the second 'consciously actualized visit' to the Grail Castle and event.

As I entered my 30s, I could say to myself: In my 20s, the gap between the given first meeting with the etheric Christ and spiritualized thinking has indeed narrowed considerably from above downward, and the bridge construction on this side was progressing successfully. However, the crucial problem concerning the spiritualization of ordinary consciousness in the physical world remained unsolved, and with it, the bridge could only be half-way completed. While I found it relatively easy to unite my imaginative cognition with spiritualized thinking, I could not find a way to spiritualize the brain-bound forces of *physical* cognition, in which earthly self-consciousness is formed. And this did not allow me to construct that part of the bridge that must lead also *from* below upward, from *physical* consciousness to imaginative consciousness. I could experience pure thinking directly in my etheric body, without going through the experience of the senses, bypassing ordinary physical cognition, but I experienced great difficulties (for example in my studies of natural science in 1976-1979) in mastering formal intellectual thinking and remembering the concrete details of sensory observations.

It was excruciatingly difficult for me to solve basic school problems of elementary maths and physics that my comrades accomplished without any effort and to fix in physical memory the results of the experiments in the lab and to grasp them with clear-cut conceptual contours and limits. I had to invest great efforts to achieve some measure of ordinary intellectual and sensory cognition that was simply the given state of consciousness to the people around me. But on the other hand, I intuitively grasped the essential ideas of each scientific discipline, that my comrades were not at all interested in. That I could kindle in each moment my spiritualized thinking and unite it with my imaginative cognition, was due to the influx of the etheric forces from the given Christ experience in the etheric world. But now I was searching for a way to develop the opposite force, that would allow me to incarnate into the physical nerve-sense system and spiritualize it. Between etheric cognition and the spiritualized thinking allied with it, and the physical brain, there was an unbridgeable abyss. But I could not find the way to generate the forces to confront and transform the forces of the physical brain, by means of which Ahriman controls modern thinking and sense-perception.

I knew that since the given Christ experience, my intuitive thinking was constantly enlivened 'from above' and was experienced in the etheric body, without passing through a fully conscious incarnation in the nerves-senses system, and without confronting, consciously, the death forces that control modern consciousness. In other words: the spiritualized thinking that I used to bring my imaginative perception to fully conscious supersensible cognition, was not flowing from the etheric to the *physical* world and back to the etheric world; it remained active in the etheric body in the etheric world; and I couldn't bring my imaginative faculties to penetrate the physical brain and transform its intellectual forces from within. I knew that in some way, I had to voluntarily 'de-spiritualize', 'devitalize', and indeed, also *kill* some of the given etheric forces and part of the given imaginative faculties. And I knew that I would have to generate the forces that would allow me to enter consciously into the physical brain and senses and ordinary consciousness based on them and spiritualize them from below upward.

This must be distinguished from the ability to work from above into the etheric body, because in this way, one reaches down only so far as to imprint in the etheric body the etheric correlates of the spiritual experiences that one investigates; but one cannot confront and overcome from above the ahrimanic forces of death in the brain, that dominate modern thinking in the physical body and world. Therefore, the problem that I faced in the second part of the first period of my life, beginning with my 30s, was no longer how to connect spiritualized thinking with imaginative perception, but how to bring down the living imaginative forces and condense them to such an extent that they could become a force of cognition inside the physical body.

What was required was a strong enough spiritual activity, to develop such intensive spiritual forces, to de-spiritualize and condense the given imaginative forces, so that—as a radically transformed spiritual force—it will penetrate the physical brain. But I could not develop this force, and I felt helpless concerning this task, even though I knew that it must be the next stage in the bridge construction. Regarding this difficult task and this deepest abyss, I remained in my divided cognitive and life situation, without being able to advance the bridge-construction work in an essential way any further.

This changed for the first time when I read again Rudolf Steiner's book *Riddles of the Soul*, written in the historical key year 1917, dedicated to the recently deceased Franz Brentano, the fine thinker and commentator on Aristotle.[45] *Riddles of the Soul* had a remarkable impact on my cognitive forces. I felt that it stimulated in my soul a new kind of spiritual activity, that I did not experience in Rudolf Steiner's works written before 1917. This new cognitive force was not only a more active force, but especially a far more *intensive*, and deeply penetrating force.

When I read the book with the forces of the Mind Soul, I experienced again an inner illumination, as I had experienced some twelve years earlier while reading *The Philosophy of Freedom* for the first time. But the meaning and direction of the two illuminations were the exact opposite. Reading *The Philosophy of Freedom*, I experienced how my free spiritual activity produces the same spiritual light that was experienced in the soul and etheric worlds, that illuminated the meeting with the etheric Christ. The illumination brought about by *Riddles of the Soul*, on the other hand, came from the opposite direction. It was experienced as a 'condensation of the light', accompanied by a certain darkening of its astral and etheric radiance. It enabled me, eventually, to *de*-spiritualize consciously part of the etheric forces and imaginative faculties, and in this form bring them to ordinary consciousness.

I felt that for the first time, through this intensive cognitive force, I would be able to form and experience ordinary intellectual thinking and brain- and sense-bound mental pictures. This was a real revelation, as if one could now accomplish something from within, voluntarily, that formerly was experienced vaguely only from

---

[45] *Von Seelenrätseln* (*Riddles of the Soul*, GA 21).

outside. This process was gaining momentum in my 33rd year of life and reached a certain culmination when I reached the 35-36th year.

After I mastered this transition from the etheric to the physical brain, on the threshold of imaginative and earthly consciousness, I could take another step. I could let go of *this* part of the etheric brain altogether and enter the physical brain, as it were, naked—to confront its death forces face to face. I could experience how the death forces suck in and destroy the forces of the etheric body in each act of physical thinking and perception. And when this confrontation was successfully accomplished, I could enter what I experienced as the grave of thinking, and not shrink back from experiencing livingly the dying process of thinking, as it is transferred from the etheric to the physical brain.

I entered consciously into this grave, as I described also in *Cognitive Yoga*, and got to know it most intimately. I could accomplish this because in my meditations I had intensified the spiritual forces generated by working with *Riddles of the Soul*; remarkably, the dying process of thinking became more alive, the more the life forces were dying; I could kill my imaginative forces and enliven the corpse of thinking, and then lift the heavy ahrimanic stone away that binds dead thinking to the brain-grave; I experienced how a new force of imagination rises 'upward' from the grave of the brain and joins the etheric body and world as a resurrected and new imaginative power.

Obviously, this process took time, and the new cognitive faculty was completed after I began my Consciousness Soul period in 1990. However, it had to be developed in the second part of the Mind Soul period to be taken over by the Consciousness Soul. Now I could experience *down here* what could never be experienced in the etheric world, namely, *the kindling of the fire and light of spiritual self-consciousness in the brain*, inside the formative forces of ordinary cognition, and experience in the *physical* world what until now could only be experienced as a given spiritual gift of the Christ in the etheric world: the formation of fully independent spiritual self-consciousness, that was an integral part of His Ego gift, but now formed solely by free spiritual activity on earth.

Understanding how the forces of death work in killing the etheric forces in the physical brain, in forming each representation and abstract concept in the intercourse with the sense-perceptible world, was a wholly new experience, about which my former experiences in the spiritual world had nothing to say. It must be first experienced consciously in the physical body and world to be known, and then we can bring its harvest with us to the spiritual world. Thanks to that part of the etheric body that could penetrate the brain to 'die and become' there, I could feel myself at home on earth for the first time, as previously, in my cognitive activity, I could feel myself at home in the soul and etheric worlds.

An important milestone on this path was experienced when I grasped concretely how ordinary sensory mental pictures and representations are formed when imaginative perception dies. What made this possible is that in *Riddles of the Soul*, Rudolf Steiner described the formation of the mental picture, the *Vorstellung*, from *both* sides of the Threshold. Perceived from the spiritual side, our representations are the result of the '*Herablähmung*', literally 'paralyzing' or 'benumbing' of the living imaginative perceptions. It is a subtle, but powerful, de-spiritualization and killing of imaginative perceptions.

This paralysis (*Herablähmung*) occurs in the formation process of each single mental picture, through which we connect dead, brain-bound thinking with perceptions and re-present living external processes as dead physical objects. Sense-perception, writes Rudolf Steiner, offers us living, ensouled and spiritual impressions, and 'of this living content man *puts to death that part which enters his ordinary consciousness*'. This was indeed experienced as the crux of the matter! It must, however, be grasped with all the intensify of spiritual consciousness and life, not as another abstract concept and dead representation. 'Man does so because he could not achieve self-consciousness if he would be immersed in the living stream of the world.' Self-consciousness, therefore, requires the killing of the living forces of the world, to separate man and make him independent. 'Without the *paralyzing of this living stream*, the human being would remain part of a world wholeness greater than his humanity; he would be an organ of a larger organism'.[46]

When I experienced myself what this passage means, it was as if a new flash of light illuminated the main riddle that had plagued my consciousness since the first meeting with the etheric Christ. It was the moment in which, for the first time, the picture of the

---

[46] *Riddles of the Soul*, 'Concerning Abstraction' (GA 21). My italics.

complete two-way bridge became visible before my soul gaze. I could see the whole human constitution, in spirit, body and soul, as the entire bridge, arched from earth to heaven and back. It was formed as a fully bridged and connected whole, in spiritual and physical self-consciousness, streaming and sparkling from above downward and from below upward, at the same time. And from that moment I dedicated myself with the greatest enthusiasm to digest and assimilate *Riddles of the Soul* and also as much as I could master of the Aristotelian way of thinking, starting from Franz Brentano and searching backward in the entwined historical paths that lead to Aristotle.

Not without significance was it also for me, at this stage, to realize—though we cannot explicate this in greater detail here—that in the same decisive year of 1917, Rudolf Steiner also hinted at the karmic significance of Brentano's Aristotelian work. He said that 'it is interesting to note how Aristotle dominated the thinking of the Middle Ages and how his philosophy was revived again by Franz Brentano and *precisely at this moment of time*. In 1911 Brentano wrote an excellent book on Aristotle in which he elaborated those ideas and concepts that he wished to bring to the attention of our present epoch. *It is a curious symptom of the Karma of our age that Brentano should have written at this precise moment of time* a comprehensive study of Aristotle which should be read by all who value a certain kind of thinking. And let me add in addition that the book is eminently readable.'[47]

In those years, I was constantly working from *Riddles of the Soul* to Brentano, from Brentano to St Thomas and Aristotle, and then back to Rudolf Steiner's new anthroposophical-Aristotelian creations. For example, for this purpose, I gathered everything Rudolf Steiner wrote and said about the mystery of the paralysis or *Herablähmung,* and his indications concerning the connections between death and consciousness and placed it in the context of the evolution of modern scientific consciousness. I tried to show that this is the common foundation of modern natural science and

---

[47] Lecture of 24 April 1917 (GA 175). My italics. Brentano's essential books on Aristotle's philosophy include also his 1867 dissertation, *The Psychology of Aristotle,* in particular his doctrine of the active intellect; *On the Several Senses of Being in Aristotle,* 1875, and *Aristoteles Lehre vom Ursprung des menschlichen Geistes* (Aristotle's Teaching on the Origin of the Human Spirit), 1911.

spiritual science. I summarized it in 1988 in an essay entitled: *Reductionism and Individuation: Interdisciplinary study of the natural scientific mode of thinking and its place in the evolution of consciousness according to the philosophical-anthroposophical investigations of Rudolf Steiner*. At this age—I had just turned 33—the inner contemplating, meditating, and researching of this process was at its most intensive stages.

Now I entered the phase of my inner development in which, based on the experience of ancient and modern Aristotelian worldviews, I also turned to the philosophy of the twentieth century. My attention was drawn to the fact that the two most significant philosophers for the development of European philosophy in the twentieth century, Edmund Husserl, the founder of the Phenomenology, and his pupil Martin Heidegger, were strongly influenced by Franz Brentano. This applies above all to Husserl who was Brentano's pupil in Vienna, in the same years in which Rudolf Steiner also visited Brentano's lectures.[48] And from Husserl the philosophic-karmic thread leads to Heidegger who became, from the end of the 1920s, a leading figure in the academic and intellectual circles of the Nazi party and movement. This intrinsically Aristotelian and scholastic stream started at the same time and place with Rudolf Steiner, while he created an anthroposophical renewal and spiritualization of Aristotle, starting with *Riddles of the Soul* in 1917. It became therefore not only a great philosophical challenge at this stage of my inner work but brought about also some difficult esoteric struggles.

Following the destiny of this stream in the first third of this century, one was led, as a matter of inner, spiritual, necessity, to great cognitive struggles with Heidegger's tempting thought, intertwined as it is in so many ways with Germany's fall into the world abyss of the 1930s and 1940s and, on the other hand, to the riddles of destiny of that significant thinker, Max Scheler, who knew Rudolf Steiner, and was Husserl's and Heidegger's original and independent collaborator, who converted to Roman Catholicism before his unexpected early death in 1928.[49]

---

[48] About the connection of Husserl's Phenomenology and Anthroposophy, see the excellent book of Scott E. Hicks, *Earthly, Transcendental, & Spiritual Logic: From Husserl's Phenomenology to Steiner's Anthroposophy* (Independently published, 2019).

[49] I described some aspects of this path in the Colmar Lecture from 2007, *Anthroposophy and Post-structural Philosophy in Dialogue* published in *Spiritual Science in the twenty-first Century* (Temple Lodge 2016).

As a result of this development, many riddles of knowledge and cognition began to be illuminated with an entirely new quality and force of thinking. And the more my studies of ancient and modern Aristotelian works and scholasticism intensified, the more I began to understand Rudolf Steiner's testamentary spiritualization of Aristotle's worldview in 1917-1924. The deeper cognitive forces of Plato and Aristotle and their historical continuation were grasped, and with them the meaning of my work in the greater context of the Michaelic School and movement at the end of the last century.

I could now understand, based on my own experience, how Rudolf Steiner characterized the difference between the thinking of Plato and Aristotle in his lecture during the Christmas Foundation Conference:

> When a modern man reads Plato with true spiritual feeling and in an attitude of meditation, after a time he begins to feel as though his head were a little higher than his physical head actually is, as though he had, so to speak, grown out beyond his physical organism. That is absolutely the experience of anyone who reads Plato, provided he does not read him in an altogether dry manner. [50]

This was part of my inborn spiritual constitution since the twenty-first year of my life, as a given faculty and through the spiritualization of thinking, by means of *The Philosophy of Freedom*, I could spiritualize it further and connect with my imaginative faculties, as described above. But now, I felt that the key was given to the riddle of the opposite stream, which allowed me in my 30s to ground, condense and incarnate my spiritual perception, and complete the bridge from both sides:

> With Aristotle it is different. With Aristotle you never have the feeling that you are coming out of your body. When you read Aristotle after having prepared yourself by meditation, you will find that he works right into the physical man. *Your physical man makes a step forward through the reading of Aristotle.* His logic works; it is not a logic that one merely observes and considers, it is a logic that works in the inner being... In a

---

[50] Lecture of 29 December 1923 (GA 233). My italics. And following quotation.

certain sense we may say with truth that Aristotle's works are only rightly comprehended when they are taken as books for meditation.

This was the decisive turning point in my spiritual development, and the foundation of the growing anthroposophical Platonic-Aristotelian synthesis. The conscious individuation of this Aristotelian spiritual force, that 'works right into the physical man', is the only way to penetrate the *physical* brain, nerves, and senses, to overcome the ahrimanic forces of death that have taken over the cosmic intelligence of Michael since the middle of the nineteenth century. I realized that I had to make this experience of death into a fully human experience, and share willingly the fate of poor Alexander, who told his teacher Aristotle: 'You are pressing together all the bones of my head!', or, as another pupil of Aristotle experienced the Aristotelian logic, as if he were thrusting his head into cold water and thereby became estranged from himself for a moment; or, as Goethe experienced it, 'there will your mind be drilled and braced/ As if in Spanish boots it were laced!'.[51] But one must voluntarily choose to suffer this Aristotelian death, also in the modern form in intellectualized anthroposophy, to spiritualize and resurrect it, and rise again from this brain-grave to unite an Aristotelian spiritualized anthroposophy with anthroposophical Platonism. And this can only be done if our heart is ablaze with the spiritualized fire that Ahriman fears most.

As a result of this experience with Aristotle's work through the centuries until today, I could also begin to be more receptive to the impact of the knowledge riddles of *Riddles of the Soul*. For example, the work with the original works of Aristotle, in connection with Brentano, especially in his *Psychology from an Empirical Standpoint* together with Rudolf Steiner's interpretation of the concept of 'intentionality' in *Riddles of the Soul*, proved immensely fruitful. My attention was sharpened considerably, and I could experience the truly unique spiritual nature of the Aristotelian forces, and how they helped me condense and incarnate my Imaginative faculties. The active spiritual force of a 'spiritualized anthroposophical Aristotelian worldview', was experienced in the sense of Rudolf Steiner's words from 1924 about the possible culmination of anthroposophy at the end of

---

[51] Lecture of 11 January 1924 (GA 233a).

the century through the new synthesis between the Aristotelian and Platonic streams. There he says, 'and so we have, I would say, working further in the anthroposophical society an Aristotelian worldview, but today in a spiritualized form, expecting its future spiritualization [at the end of the twentieth century]'.[52] I could experience this with great intensity from the middle of the 1980s until the middle of the 1990s, as described in the second lecture in *The Twilight and Resurrection of Humanity*.

To appreciate the nature of the essence exchange between the Platonic and Aristotelian spiritual forces, it is helpful to get acquainted with the picture given by Rudolf Steiner at the beginning of the book *Riddles of the Soul*. It was used again and again in my meditations in this period of my development. This picture describes the way in which supersensible cognition reaches down and crosses the Threshold from above downwards, and how it meets there the highest forces of ordinary human cognition that ascend to the Threshold from below. I found that my innermost soul—and spirit situation, standing, as described above, on the edge of the uncompleted 'bridge' of my divided existence, was described faithfully in this picture:

> In that Anthroposophy advances from experiences of the spiritual world outside of the human being, to the human being, it finds, eventually, the human being that lives in the sense-body and developing in this body a consciousness of sense-reality. The last thing that it finds in the human being on its way down, is the soul being with its living mental pictures. This it can describe with coherent imaginative pictures. Then it can still use the spiritual gaze—at the end of the path of spiritual research—to see how the essential life of the mental pictures is suppressed [*abgelähmt, herabgelähmt*] by sense-perception. In this suppressed life of mental pictures, it illuminates, from the spiritual side, the human being that lives in the sense-world, in so far as he is a thinking being.

It is there, so to say, that the lungs and heart of the knowledge drama of the Second Coming breathe and pulse, expand in a Platonic way upward and contract in an Aristotelian way downwards, inhaling and exhaling with Michael's Yoga will, and on passing through each

---

[52] Lecture of 18 July 1924 (GA 240).

other, offer the other a potent seed essence of itself, interchangeably; there it must be grasped and condensed:

> If we go in both ways, the anthroposophical and the anthropological correctly, *so they meet together in one point...* those that observe the two ways... shall achieve with their mental pictures a fitting-together similar to the one found between the positive and negative plate images of a photographed picture. [53]

When this living essence exchange was well established, a new challenge emerged, that must be pointed out as well. After a certain balance between the Platonic and Aristotelian forces was achieved, it tipped over to the materialistic side, as an opposite mirror picture of the fact that previously my forces were centred in the spiritual side. It seemed that the forces of old and new Aristotelism and intellectualism, that brought the knowledge drama thus far, became too strong. I found myself engaged in a soul-desolating fight with the decadent, fallen forces of the modern ahrimanic intellect. This struggle became now inevitable. I realized that my engagement with natural science and academic philosophy also contributed to this tipping of the balance downward.

From the middle of the Mind Soul period, I had to increasingly face the impact of modern, ahrimanic intellectualism and materialism. But I felt that this was an inevitable part of the bridge construction, and that the struggle with these forces of death is necessary, to develop the forces to overcome Ahriman's strongest influence. The spiritual forces from the Platonic source were always available, but by themselves they could not fulfil this task, and I felt that some help must be found from the Aristotelian side, because I had to develop the strongest spiritual forces of spiritualized Aristotelism itself. Therefore, I was searching for the pertinent 'road sign' to direct me in this new crucial turn of the path, but some difficult times of wanderings were required before such help was vouchsafed.

The new guidance came unexpectedly, in two steps. The first was found in Walter Johannes Stein's book on the Grail in the

---

[53] *Riddles of the Soul*, Chapter 1, 'Anthropology and Anthroposophy' (GA 21). My italics. This meeting together in 'one point' is the heart organ, formed by the indwelling 'I' of Christ, through the essence exchange and metamorphosis of Plato and Aristotle.

ninth century. I found there a reference to the connection between Aristotelism and the Grail stream in the past, that gave me an important clue to search for the present connection. One important indication was about what could have happened in the past:

> What a turning in human history could occur if the mysteries of antiquity, gathered in Aristotelism, could fully enter the Persian cultural element, renewed through Manichaeism. [54]

Above we pointed out the significance of Rudolf Steiner's lecture cycle in Berlin, in March-April 1917: *Building Stones to the Understanding of the Mystery of Golgotha*. In the lecture dedicated to Aristotle's spiritual path, we find also this indication concerning Emperor Julian. 'The aim of Manichaeism was the conquest of evil and of matter by thought. Julian was brought face to face with the deeper implications of the problem of evil and the relation of Christ Jesus to this problem. He hoped to find an answer through initiation into the Persian Mysteries and to return to Europe with the solution.' [55] This directive was now confirmed in Stein's indication, when he characterized the relation of Aristotelism, in this sense, to the Christ impulse:

> The thinking of Aristotle has the power to spiritualize matter and evil. This is the reason why Christianity took into itself the thought of Aristotle because the centre of the Christian mystery, the transubstantiation of matter in the Mass, can only be understood by means of Aristotelian thinking.[56]

I felt that Stein was pointing my attention towards an essential aspect of future Aristotelism, that has much to do with the formation of ordinary consciousness through the dying of the given imaginative consciousness and its conscious resurrection in modern supersensible cognition, that constitute the centre of the knowledge drama of the Second Coming. And then came the second hint, that indicated the place I had been searching for during that time. It was a most essential 'road sign' at this juncture of the path. This 'sign' was found in Stein's philosophical Ph.D. Dissertation, that in 1985 was made available for

---

[54] W.J. Stein, *The Ninth Century and the Holy Grail* (p 113).
[55] Lecture of 19 April 1917 (GA 175).
[56] W. J Stein, ibid. p. 117.

the first time since 1921.[57] This happened in the moment in which I found myself in 'the middle of my path', exactly in the middle point between the original, given meeting with the Christ, and the second, consciously individualized meeting. As Thomas Meyer shows in his fine commentary, Stein was writing his dissertation under the personal guidance of Rudolf Steiner and was striving to create a seed for 'a knowledge theory of the higher stages of supersensible cognition'. It was written during Stein's service in the First World War, while Rudolf Steiner developed what came to light in *Riddles of the Soul* in 1917, and I experienced it as a vital addendum to this book.

In a very special way (described in the 2nd lecture of *The Twilight and Resurrection of Humanity*), Stein became an energetic spiritual companion on this path and helped me locate and actualize the missing link in the construction of the bridge, when the crossing point of the middle was tipping in the ahrimanic direction. It made it possible to find the path that leads directly to the conscious confrontation with the mystery of death, that lies at the foundation of modern cognition and consciousness.

I needed the key to this mystery of death to fulfil the spiritual development of my Mind Soul in the 1980s, to complete the two-way bridge between the etheric and physical worlds, between the new revelation of the etheric Christ and the free spiritual activity of spiritual science. I realized how this form of anthroposophical Aristotelism, 'in the person who is developing spiritually the Consciousness Soul, is transformed into the Imagination Soul [...] and the Consciousness Soul makes use of the brain of the physical body ... the Imagination Soul actually enters into the physical body and permeates it'.[58] And further, I could experience what it meant in practice, that 'occult training will, by the transformation of the physical body, show the Mystery of the Living Christ in a new way'.[59] This realization finally allowed me to bring together all my cognitive efforts from the first part of my life and create the bridging knowledge drama of the Second Coming at the end of the twentieth century.

---

[57] *W.J Stein / Rudolf Steiner-Dokumentation eines wegweisenden Zusammenwirkens* (Verlag am Goetheanum, 1985).

[58] Lecture of 29 March 1913 (GA 145). In Chapter 5 of *The New Experience of the Supersensible* this process is described in detail from various points of view.

[59] Lecture of 17 June 1910 (GA 121).

Let me say this in a straightforwardly and radical manner—that, however, fully accords with the facts. Aristotle's unique spirit force became my intimate guide to 'kill' the inborn Platonic faculties and resurrect them to new life, permeated and transformed by the new forces of the presently active Aristotelian power. This was a service of love, of course, because it was a Michaelic deed in the service of Christ. I had to thank Aristotle's Michaelic power for the experience of *In Christo Morimur*, that enabled me to confront the ahrimanic forces of death that rule the intellect, and resurrect them in the etheric heart, through the life forces of the etheric Christ; only this force could open the conscious way to confront the ahrimanic forces that dominate our modern intellect. Only the spiritualized Aristotelism that Rudolf Steiner added to the development of spiritual science after 1917, could support the overcoming and resurrection of the death-bringing ahrimanic intellectualism.

In these years, I felt the need, in my meditations, to contemplate again and again, how Rudolf Steiner himself experienced the creation of *The Riddles of the Soul*. He said that this book 'is not written with the pen, but with spiritual spades that want to tear down the boards that seal the world, that is, to eliminate the limits of the knowledge of nature, but to eliminate them through inner soul work... What is written in this first chapter of *The Riddles of the Soul* is the attempt to smash these boards away... with which the world has been sealed for centuries, with spades'.[60] And we experienced with inner shudder the tragic karma of humanity in the twentieth century, in Rudolf Steiner's untiring effort to spiritualize the Aristotelian impulse, with which his individual karma is intimately connected, when we realize that when the book was published, in the autumn of 1917, he already said that 'in many things that are written in this way for the present, one already has the feeling that one writes something testamentary'.[61]

The overcoming of the ahrimanic intellect, and its resurrection through the etheric Christ forces, made it possible to anchor the bridge also on the *physical* side of the River of Lethe. One could become a conscious worker also on the physical side of the bridge and direct its construction from both directions simultaneously. Now it was possible to find the best spiritual practice to proceed towards the meeting point of the two streams from both sides of the

---

[60] Lecture of 4 February 1923 (GA 221).
[61] Lecture of 7 October 1917 (GA 177).

Threshold. At this stage of the work, the central task was to transfer the unique spiritual forces, extracted from the 'spiritualized anthroposophical Aristotelism' in the physical body, to the etheric body and the given imaginative faculties.

The key to fulfil this task was discovered when it was realized that this intensive Aristotelian spiritual extract, harvested in the overcoming of Ahriman in the physical body and cognition, added a wholly new and special force to the etheric body. This special etheric force was now on the same level as the despiritualized Platonic etheric forces. The Aristotelian etheric force was spiritualized and extracted from the physical body below and was now led upward to the etheric body; the Platonic spiritual forces, coming from above, were condensed in the etheric body. Both could now mutually interpenetrate and enhance each other in the etheric body. The middle etheric crossing point between them could be found and actualized in imaginative perception, cognition, and spiritual self-consciousness.

In other words, I discovered something that had far-reaching consequences for the entire development of the knowledge drama, namely, that *the new anthroposophical Aristotelism could accomplish in the etheric body what the original Aristotelism accomplished in the physical body.* In the etheric body it could merge with the imaginative Platonic forces, and help them to condense further, etherically speaking. What is more, this etheric concentration and condensation developed the forces of supersensible cognition beyond the Imaginative Soul. I discovered that in this way the forces of the Imaginative Soul, the spiritualized Consciousness Soul, were transformed. The forces of the Imaginative Soul became saturated with inspired and intuited forces, that later could develop into the forces of the Inspirative—and Intuitive Souls, described in greater detail in *The New Experience of the Supersensible.* I found out that paradoxically, when this ahrimanic force that causes the killing of spiritual perception and its paralysis ('*harablähmung*') into ordinary representations, is spiritualized, it has the opposite effect. It saturated the original imaginative perception with inspired and intuited forces, from which the bridge could receive its necessary solid etheric forces and substances. An enhanced imaginative faculty was the result, that could perceive in real time, simultaneously, the downward and upward streaming formative spiritual currents, and could hold them at their crossing point, through which the bridge could be finally completed.

I said to myself in those years, when I repeatedly contemplated the results of this special force, that certainly it continued to work ('*Es arbeitet*') powerfully onward. This unique Aristotelian secret force at the end of the twentieth century, was proving its fruitfulness in achieving the same consistency and concentrating power of cognition, but now not in the 'physical human being' but in the 'etheric human being'. The same Aristotelian spiritual energy, that led humanity 2500 years ago, as a matter of evolutionary and karmic necessity, from the remnants of ancient imaginative cognition—still present in Plato and the Platonic teachers of Chartres—down to the new logical-physical, earth-bound, dead thinking, at the end of the twentieth century has the task, through the same evolutionary and karmic necessity, to unite again with spiritualized, anthroposophical Platonism, that could spiritualize it further. And this spiritualized Aristotelianism, in turn, could condense the spiritual forces of Platonism, concentrate, and saturate the new imaginative perception.

I could feel that what I experienced was justified, because it answered Rudolf Steiner's hopeful indication concerning the possible culmination of anthroposophy at the end of the last century. As I showed in *The Twilight and Resurrection of Humanity*, in 1924 Rudolf Steiner hoped for an earthly incarnation of all the Platonic and Aristotelian souls, to work together on earth for the first time at the end of the century. The result of this 'culmination' would be that the spiritualization of 'anthroposophical Aristotelism', began at the beginning of the century, 'awaiting its further spiritualization', would be greatly intensified. 'That which today can shine as if only through tiny windows must, in the future, become a unity through the coming together of the leaders of the School of Chartres and the leading spirits of Scholasticism, when at the end of the twentieth century that spiritual renewing will come to pass whereby intellectualism is lifted to the spirit.'[62]

---

[62] Lecture of 18 July 1924 (GA 240). In my book *The Twilight and Resurrection of Humanity: The History of the Michaelic Movement since the Death of Rudolf Steiner. An Esoteric Study*, I showed that at the end of the century the stream of Michael could once more only 'shine through tiny windows', because only a small group of Platonic souls incarnated on earth, supported by those Aristotelian souls that remained loyal to Michael. The Platonic task was nevertheless to 'lift intellectualism to the spirit' and bring about a further spiritualization of Aristotelism.

As shown in detail in Chapters 4 and 5 of *The New Experience of the Supersensible*, this problem is central to the transition from the given supersensible 'percept' to the spiritual-scientific 'concept' that belongs to it as the knowledge drama of the Second Coming. The new anthroposophical Aristotelism could help bring about the incarnation of anthroposophical Platonism, from the etheric to the physical world, where it could use the new life forces streaming from the etheric Christ, to confront and overcome the death forces of the ahrimanic intellect. In this way 'the Imaginative Soul [could] enter the physical body and permeate it', and through the etherized brain and heart forces return it to Michael. At the same time, anthroposophical Aristotelism was spiritualized and lifted to the etheric world, and one could apply its intense forces to concentrate and condense the imaginative faculties working in the etheric body, and in this way complete the formation of the two-way bridge in the etheric body. Goethe's *Green Snake* bridge in the etheric body was thus completed and could open the way to the knowledge drama of the Second Coming.

This means that the energetic synergy and essence exchange between the two streams allowed them to cross and reverse themselves in and through each other: the Platonic stream could incarnate into the physical body and the Aristotelian could excarnate to the etheric body. And when one grasped them 'at the etheric point of their crossing', according to Dionysius' and Michael's Yoga breathing, at the crossing point one experienced the full scope of the hoped for 'culmination' at the end of the twentieth century, the synthesis and synergy of anthroposophical Aristotelism and Platonism; this could be experienced, on earth, according to the new Michaelic agreement and plan, to begin with only from the *Platonic* side, but in doing so, it paved the way for the possible future incarnation of the stream of Michael, according to the new Michaelic plan, described in *The Twilight and Resurrection of Humanity*.

This mutual essence exchange transformed both, bringing anthroposophical Platonism one level lower, to a fully conscious imaginative perception and cognition inside the physical forces of the brain and sense-nerve system, and raised anthroposophical Aristotelism one level higher, to the etheric world and imaginative cognition. And through this new imaginative cognition one could grasp the new revelation of the etheric Christ in a conscious way, through the meetings with the beings of Michael and Anthroposophia.

I said to myself often at this stage, that only in such a conscious way would it be possible to confront the forces of death, and that this confrontation alone could generate the forces required to overcome and spiritualize them. One must die first into the abyss of the brain, to find there—inside the mystery of death—the forces of resurrection. And that only during this practice can we realize Paul's secret of esoteric Christianity; this can only be discovered in the practice itself. To say it briefly in this Prelude to *The New Experience of the Supersensible*, where it is reported in greater detail: if we livingly, that is, consciously, die into the forces of death, the forces of life—given by the etheric Christ—while dying, resurrect these forces of death and lift them to the etheric body. The sacrifice of the forces of life transfers them into the forces of death, and then the forces of death become alive, while the formerly living forces die.

As a matter of fact, what takes place is a most remarkable essence exchange between Christ's life and the death forces taken into Christ. The life forces offer their abundant life to death, that has a great lack, an abyssal minus of life, and when death is tempted to take them into itself, it must assimilate them, and unwittingly enters into a most intimate wedding with Christ's life. So when Christ dies in us, death begins to live, but for death to live means, essentially—from its point of view—to die; so when Christ dies in our death forces, death in us dies too, but it dies in Christ's death, which means, it dies into infinitely abundant life: it is resurrected through Christ's life. We experience what it really means that in the Mystery of Golgotha, 'Christ espoused death', as Rudolf Steiner said;[63] it becomes reality, and the secret of esoteric Christianity is consciously grasped and individualized.

Furthermore, when we observe the results of this mysterious essence exchange in the etheric body, we discover that the resurrected force of death constitutes new etheric forces, different from the given etheric forces. They add a new etheric force to them that was not there before, and enhances the supersensible faculties of perception. And the force of resurrected death added to the etheric body has two related aspects: first, it spiritualizes further the given etheric forces and the imaginative cognition based on them, and second, they become the *spiritual* formative force that constitutes the foundation of *spiritual* self-consciousness outside the

---

[63] Lecture of 6 July 1909 (GA 112).

physical body. And we experience that this allows the two states of self-consciousness to unite: the self-consciousness given with the 'I' of Christ in the etheric world, streaming from above, and earthly self-consciously formed in the physical brain, that rises from the physical body below. Where the two meet and exchange their spiritual essences with each other, the bridge can be fully formed. This becomes its most fundamental basis and anchorage, in both worlds. And what is more, we could experience already in the first stages of this process how the forces of imaginative perception, that became stronger, also penetrate our daily consciousness. And though biographically speaking this would not be fully accomplished before the Consciousness Soul forces would begin to develop freely at the age of 35-6, the first rays of this dawn became perceptible at that time. One could therefore hope to eventually achieve distinctly separated and wholly integrated spiritual and physical states of consciousness, that would mutually enhance and illuminate each other.

At this time of my life and development, the above-described mystery of 'die and become' became intensively alive in my thinking, feeling and will forces. In my meditations, I contemplated the bridge-building process in its entirety, in which the knowledge drama of the Second Coming would be realized. I said to myself, when I wished to place the essence of this process in the centre of my heart: Through the given Ego of the etheric Christ your spiritual 'I' was born in the spiritual world. *Ex Deo Nascimur*. But you willingly took the death forces of the brain into the forces of this birth, the moment you entered physical consciousness. You must find a way to assimilate the forces of birth and death into the Christ forces in the etheric heart, and pray that if life becomes death, death will become life as well: *In Christo Morimur*; and then you experience the third mystery, how the resurrected forces of death light up in Christ, to become a source of fresh spiritual light and sight, that illuminate the completed bridge: *Per Spiritum Sanctum Reviviscimus*. This became my daily meditation when I reached my 33rd year of life, in the crucial years of the first part of my life, in which the knowledge drama and bridge construction would require the greatest intensity of spiritual activity.

This work, accomplished at the end of the last century, makes the whole bridge visible and available to each person who seeks it in the twenty-first century. It appears as a living, shining, etheric bridge, connecting, in modern self-consciousness, the physical and spiritual worlds. Through this etheric bridge, the revelation of the etheric Christ and the present Michaelic impulse is grasped in exact and clear imaginative cognition. What made the actualization of the bridge-building process possible, in the actual, practical, spiritual-scientific praxis, was the ability to locate and grasp exactly the place where the two streams meet, cross each other, and exchange their spiritual essences with each other; and then, to hold this point and this essence exchange firmly, through the etheric breathing activity of the etheric head, heart and limbs, as we showed in *Cognitive Yoga*. In this way, it was possible to grasp and actualize the crossing point and essence exchange between the two opposite spirit streams and movements: the bridge of self-conscious continuation of imaginative *and* ordinary consciousness was built, and the spiritualized forces of earthly cognition, streaming upward, exchanged its forces with the forces of the despiritualized imaginative cognition streaming downward. This powerful essence exchange at the end of the twentieth century was indeed an exact karmic inversion of what took place between Aristotle and Plato in the past:

> Now there came a very important turning-point, which is expressed very clearly and even historically in the transition from Plato to Aristotle. It is remarkable that, in the evolution of this Greek civilization, as the fourth century began, this first transition towards the abstract appeared. This fact is exemplified in the following scene which took place between Plato and Aristotle, at a time when Plato was very old, and really at the end of his earthly career. I must of course clothe in words what naturally occurred in a much more complicated way. Plato said to Aristotle somewhat as follows: 'Many things I have told you and my other pupils may not have seemed correct to you, but what I have told you is really an extract of the most ancient holy Mystery-Wisdom. Human beings will, however, in the course of their evolution acquire such a form and such an inner organization, which will gradually lead them to something certainly higher than we now possess but this will at the same time make it impossible for them to accept natural science in the way it is presented to the Greeks.' Plato made this clear to Aristotle. *'Therefore, I will withdraw myself for a time'*, said Plato, *'and will leave you to yourself.* In the world of thought, for which

> you are so especially endowed, and which will become the
> thought-world of humanity for many centuries, try to build up
> in thoughts what you have learned here in my school.' So Plato
> and Aristotle separated, and Plato therewith fulfilled, as com-
> manded, a high spiritual mission through Aristotle.[64]

We know from Rudolf Steiner's karma lecture from 23 September,
1924 that also at the end of the nineteenth century the reincarnated
Plato, as Karl Julius Schröer, 'withdrew himself' again, 'and left
Rudolf Steiner to himself', but now this withdrawal was not done in
the service of Michael, which demanded the spiritualization of the
modern natural-scientific intellect; and therefore, as a result of this
omission, Rudolf Steiner had to take Schröer's mission on himself.[65]

Karmically speaking, it is not without significance, that as the
result of the new Michaelic plan and agreement in the middle of the
twentieth century, it was the task of anthroposophical Platonism to
take on itself what anthroposophical Aristotelism failed to accomplish at the beginning of the century. And this task was to create the
self-conscious and modern, thought permeated and exact, imaginative cognition, to fulfil the new anthroposophical impulse at the
end of the twentieth and beginning of the twenty-first centuries.

Looking now back at this work, that was accomplished some 35
years ago, I can say to myself: Indeed, I didn't 'give up the drama of
knowledge in favour of the grammar of knowledge'. I can say that
'also the fear didn't hold me back, that I might fall into the abyss
of individuation'. I sought this abyss consciously, and when it was
found, I went down its steep cognitive slopes in full consciousness,
because I trusted that I would find again—in a new way, in the
abyss—the forces of resurrection, and 'arise out of this abyss united
with many spirits, and experience myself in kinship with them', as
happened in the community that I could create in the twenty-first
century in the new school of spiritual science. I could experience it
as my individualized knowledge drama of the Second Coming and
create the pearl of greatest spiritual price in those dark ahrimanic
depths, in the only place it can be created in our time. 'So is man
born out of the spiritual world'—this spiritual birth was, as shown
above, the conscious starting point, as a given gift, in the meeting
with the etheric Christ; but what I had to accomplish, by means of

---

[64] Lecture of 14 December 1923 (GA 232). My italics.
[65] Lecture of 23 September 1924 (GA 238).

my free spiritual forces, was 'to take in Death and become myself, in a spiritual way, the annihilator of the becoming'. This was the turning point on the path, described above; this was the decisive point, the individuation of Christ's given 'I', the only 'I' that can 'take in death and become the annihilator of the becoming, and be present in its annihilation'. This meant to become fully conscious and present in 'time's annihilating stream', as the opening verse of the First Class says, in the annihilation of primordial divine becoming, go through this death in full consciousness, and let 'not "I" but the indwelling "I" of Christ', resurrect my 'I'.

I felt that I could individualize in this way the essence of Rudolf Steiner's description of the knowledge drama. 'Man should not give up the drama of knowledge in favour of the grammar of knowledge; also, the fear that he might fall into the abyss of individuation must not hold him back, because man arises out of this abyss united with many spirits, and experiences himself in kinship with them. So is man born out of the spiritual world, but he took in Death, became himself the annihilator of the becoming, experiences it in a spiritual way and is present in its annihilation.'[66]

This is possible today due to the new life forces flowing from both Mysteries of Golgotha, the physical and etheric mysteries of death and resurrection, which the etheric Christ is offering today in His 'I' gift. Then the resurrected and redeemed forces of death become 'the forces of eternal soul awakening', because, when we learn how to individualize and actualize this mystery, we will experience 'having-death-beside-us as something natural' and learn how 'to awaken in oneself the powers of eternal soul alertness', and this means, 'to have death as a good friend and constant companion always by one's side'.[67]

The books, *The New Experience of the Supersensible*, *The Spiritual Event of the 20th Century*, and *The Twilight and Resurrection of Humanity*, can only be understood if we realize that they contain the new teaching of the resurrected *etheric* Christ. The result of this teaching is the 'resurrection of direct Christ consciousness', resurrected in the second Mystery of Golgotha, in fully awakened *earthly* consciousness. As the resurrected Christ taught His disciples after

---

[66] *Wahrspruchworte* (GA 40, 1923). About the knowledge drama, see also the lecture of 5 November 1917 (GA 73).
[67] Lecture 9 September 1924 (GA 346).

Golgotha the mysteries of His *physical* death and resurrection, so at the end of the twentieth century He taught them the mysteries of His *etheric* death and resurrection.[68] The knowledge drama of the Second Coming, described in *The New Experience of the Supersensible*, Christ's sacrifice through the apocalyptic history of the twentieth century, described in *The Spiritual Event of the 20th century*, and His resurrection in the new Michaelic Christ revelation of the twenty-first century, described in *The Twilight and Resurrection of Humanity*, is the summary of the teachings given by the resurrected etheric Christ. He could give this teaching after he completed the *century-long* second Mystery of Golgotha, because of what He experienced in His etheric death from the end of the nineteenth until the end of the twentieth century, leading to His etheric resurrection at the beginning of the twenty-first century.

---

[68] About the teaching of the physically resurrected Christ, see the lecture of 13 April 1922 (GA 211).

Chapter 4
The Meeting with the Etheric Christ

The given meeting with the Christ is described in Chapter 4 of *The New Experience of the Supersensible*, 'The Modern Christ Experience— The Meeting with the New Initiator'. As we showed in the Introduction, if man illuminates this meeting with the light of spiritual science, he will realize that the Christ offers the human 'I' a seed, or 'copy', of His 'I', that contains three golden spiritual seeds of future transformation and development. He plants the three seeds in the human spirit, soul, and body, as a gift of grace. But the Christ doesn't only give a copy of His 'I', He also accompanies the gift with an exemplary demonstration of what man can do with it, if he would freely choose to individualize the given 'I' in his free 'I' and meet the Christ voluntarily. In the actual experience, the 'I' gift and the three seeds and stages form a unity but are described separately for the sake of clarity.

The first stage plants a golden spirit seed of resurrection and awakening of *spiritual cognition* in the forces of death that dominate human consciousness in the present age. This happens through the *Imagination* of Christ's etheric *appearance.* The second golden spirit seed contains the forces of healing of the *wounded human heart and fragmented soul forces* and is planted through the *Inspiration* of His living *words.* The third golden spirit seed is a triumphant spirit flame that kindles the eternal fire of the 'I' inside the *physical body.* This happens through the *Intuition* of His active *presence and deeds.*

These imaginative, inspirative and intuitive experiences are the revelations of the etheric Christ that appears, speaks, and acts as a Sun Being, and the clear differentiation between them is made possible through the knowledge drama of the Second Coming, outlined below. In this Prelude, we briefly describe some aspects of the first stage of the meeting, in which a significant transformation of consciousness takes place. We can understand the nature of this transformation if we compare it to our ordinary consciousness.

In daily life, we have self-consciousness as a given fact in the physical world, but we have no consciousness of our spiritual 'I'. When we incarnate in the physical body we develop physical self-consciousness, and give up our spiritual consciousness, that remains in a state of deep unconscious sleep during earthly life. In the moment the human 'I' faces Christ's 'I' in the etheric world, and an imprint of Christ's 'I' is implanted in man's 'I', these two separate states become one. Our physical self-consciousness is raised from the physical body and world to the etheric body and world, but doesn't dissolve there, as happens in sleep and after death. Through the power of the given 'I' of Christ, it becomes *spiritual* self-consciousness, and man experiences his 'I' as an independent spiritual self in the etheric world in all clarity of spiritual self-consciousness, as distinct and light-filled as our ordinary physical self-consciousness.

We must imagine, therefore, a wholly new spiritual situation and event, in which we find ourselves in this meeting. This new situation is an intensive etheric event, and the world in which it is constituted and grounded is the etheric world. *Supersensible self-consciousness is the new state of consciousness constituted in this event.* That is, in this meeting, the two states of consciousness are fused together, that are mutually exclusive on earth, and create a third and wholly new state of consciousnesses: *self-conscious spiritual consciousness.* The ordinary fully awake self-consciousness and the unconscious spiritual consciousness, entirely separated from each other in modern life, merge with each other, and their essences are mutually exchanged and transformed. The unconscious spiritual consciousness becomes self-conscious, and physical self-consciousness becomes spiritualized. As the given 'I' of Christ and the 'I' of man interpenetrate, also both states of consciousnesses penetrate each other, and each is transformed through the other. This essence exchange occurs in the giving and receiving of Christ's Ego-copy, and the light that brings it to full spiritual self-consciousness is the 'light of the Grail', the light of modern spiritual science.[69]

---

[69] As was pointed out in the Introduction, 'through seeing the Holy Grail, [we] get to know the mystery of the Christ-Ego... [and] receive the Christ-Ego at the sight of the Holy Grail'. (Lecture of 11 April 1909, GA 109.) As we shall see below, the spiritual source of this light becomes known only later, during further spiritual scientific investigations, and is revealed as the beings of Michael and Anthroposophia. To begin with, however, this light, that illuminates the meeting with the Christ, is given as an integral part of the given event, and we do not distinguish it from the whole occurrence.

The spiritualization of self-consciousness also radically transforms our perception and understanding of what the 'I' really is.
In the physical world, I know about my 'I' only what the body and
senses reveal to me, and therefore I know that this 'I' is but an illu-
sory reflection of the body and will perish with the body at death.
But now one becomes conscious of the fact that the 'I' is a universal,
indeed, cosmic, spiritual being, and is part of the spiritual world.
And as the physical world, with its forces and substances, builds
and shapes the physical body, through which we gain our ordinary
self-consciousness, so does the Christ in the etheric world regarding our etheric body and the new state of spiritual self-consciousness. That is, when we face the etheric Christ and He offers His 'I'
to us, we experience how the objective supersensible reality—in the
centre of which the Christ appears—becomes the formative force of
spiritual self-consciousness that, until now, could only exist in the
physical world.

As the physical world gives us physical self-consciousness as a
given gift, the etheric Christ in the etheric world gives us the seed
of spiritual self-consciousness as a given gift. This etheric, imaginative, self-consciousness is a new state of consciousness, gracefully
offered by Christ's imaginative appearance, words and deeds, and
this is the reason why the giving and receiving of His Ego takes
place in the most lucid, clear, and self-conscious imaginative perception. And the knowledge drama of the Second Coming is the
active individualization and recapitulation of this offer of the Ego
and the formation of spiritual self-consciousness.

If we want to portray this situation and event accurately, from
the point of view of modern spiritual science, we must say: In the
imaginatively perceived world a Being appears—the only one of
this kind in our world—through whose etheric appearance, words
and deeds, that takes place between His 'I' and the human 'I', the
totality of the Idea, the divine archetype of man, in spirit, soul and
body, is directly perceived. We experience and see, through the
appearance, words, and deeds of the 'I' of Christ in our own 'I',
the future wholeness and fullness of our divine nature; it appears
spread out in everlasting time, as an entire stream of becoming,
from the remotest past to the far future.

Therefore, in this meeting, during the giving and receiving of
Christ's 'I', we are not external onlookers as in the physical world.
Because our true 'I' is given to us, we participate inwardly and

actively in this event; it is a dynamic, breathing, and reciprocal event between the divine 'I' of Christ and the human 'I'; we know that the Being who appears in the external, objective, etheric world, is our Higher Self, the representative of humanity. We are lifted at this moment out of our physical body and ordinary consciousness and are taken gracefully into His being, and at the same time we take in—etherically speaking—His Ego, offered through His etheric appearance, words and deeds.

As shown also in Chapter 10 of *Cognitive Yoga*, this is a mutual becoming: the Christ takes the essence of our earthly being into His divine 'I' and we take the seed of His 'I' into our earthly being. In the kindled spiritual self-consciousness, we become part of His eternal being and becoming; and through His 'I' planted in our earthly being, He becomes an eternal part of us. And we know that this event is not a mere personal event; we experience it as microcosmic reflection of cosmic happening, and we realize that we become active and creative etheric participants in the becoming process of the cosmos, in the wide-open etheric world. We feel that the whole universe participates with us and through us in this human-world becoming process, and we know: through the given 'I' of the etheric Christ we have been given a precious golden spirit seed, and if we nourish and cultivate it properly, individualize and develop it through spiritual science, we can realize the infinite becoming process of our future humanity, because this 'I' embodies the divine archetype and fullness of our entire future human-cosmic becoming.

Let us make clear to ourselves how different the experience of the etheric world is from the experience of the physical world and how differently we experience ourselves in our etheric body in the etheric world than in our physical body in the physical world. The two worlds and experiences are reversed in essential respects. In the physical world we feel that we are outside the things that we observe and represent to ourselves. In the etheric world all processes, events and beings interpenetrate each other and interpenetrate also our etheric being and consciousness. Also, in the physical world, things and objects preserve their forms intact in space and time, but in the etheric world all things exist in perpetual change, movement and becoming.

When we find ourselves in this world, as happens in the given Christ experience, or when we raise ourselves to this world by means of our spiritual activity, we merge and become one with its abundant life, and are transformed and changed, with each being, event and process that we encounter. We are always becoming something and someone else in the etheric world, and this *becoming other* through constant metamorphosis, is the only true sense of 'being' in this world. In the physical world, becoming has come to a final halt in fixed being, and in the etheric world true being *is* becoming. There is absolutely no fixed and separate being in this stream of perpetual becoming.

And if this is true for each single being and process, we must realize to what extent this applies to the appearance, words, and deeds of the etheric Christ. He appears as the cosmic heart centre and life fountain of the world of etheric becoming; *He is the being of infinite becoming*; His etheric appearance, words and deeds consist of perpetual actualization of metamorphosis, transformation, change and growth. And this is the spiritual essence of the 'I' that He gives us. Therefore, if we want to investigate this experience and recapitulate it voluntarily, we must *become His becoming*, in a conscious way. The threefold spiritual meeting with the Christ: His imaginative appearance, inspirative words and intuitive deeds, not only demonstrate the objective becoming process of humanity and the earth, but His 'I' demonstrates it through and inside our 'I'. He is therefore the supreme teacher of the mutual human world becoming in our universe. This means that our spiritualized cognitive activity is not taking place outside the being that we know, but inside this being, and our cognition is spiritualized by means of the force of spiritual becoming that flows from this being, the etheric Christ.

We know Him through the light of His freely given Ego; it is His 'I' who knows Himself in our 'I', and He offers us as a gift of grace the light of His cosmic-human self-knowledge. This is the essence exchange between man and Christ, through which His 'I' becomes our 'I', and we become a spiritual 'I' in Him.[70] And when we search for the concept that characterizes this essence exchange in the etheric world most precisely, a concept that can most readily be understood in physical life, we find it in the fundamental life process of breathing. Spiritual breathing becomes, therefore, a

---

[70] As described also in Chapter 10 of *Cognitive Yoga*: 'Essence exchange with the Cosmic Source'. (Temple Lodge, 2016.)

bridging experience, that helps us to form the voluntary path to the etheric Christ, based on the Michaelic Yoga described above, actualized in the knowledge drama of the Second Coming.

Our physical senses, eyes, ears, smell, taste and touch, balance, movement, and life are part of the physical body, by means of which we become external onlookers; we observe things and processes in the external world in our own body and make representations about them in our separated mind. But imaginative perception and cognition is a living and breathing, pulsating, immanent activity, through which we *become one with what we perceive.* And the life process par excellence of becoming, already in the physical world, is the rhythmic, perpetual, and reciprocal process of *breathing.*

In the physical world we breathe in three distinct and separate ways: we exchange gases with the air, we assimilate, digest, and excrete foodstuffs taken from the physical world, and we represent the world by means of the intake of sense-perceptions. But in the etheric world the three processes of breathing, nourishment and perception are one and the same life process. In our etheric breathing, what we know is what gives us new life, energizes, and nourished us, and builds our cognition and body at the same time, because the whole etheric body is a body of imaginative cognition. Breathing, nourishment, and knowledge is one and the same life-knowledge-substance-giving process in the etheric world, by exchanging purely etheric streams, forces, and processes with the whole etheric cosmos and earth.

More pictorially expressed, we can also portray this process of etheric breathing as follows. In the etheric world we 'inhale' the threefold gift of Christ's 'I', through His etheric appearance, words, and deeds, into our self-conscious 'I', soul and bodily forces. Then by means of the forces that we received from Him, we 'exhale' our spiritual, soul, and bodily activity and forces to unite again with His etheric being. As the plant breathes in light, warmth and air from the sun and the whole surrounding atmosphere, so do we breathe in His etheric forces, to transform ourselves into a self-conscious 'I' in the etheric world, into active soul beings, and resurrected bodily beings; and as the plant breathes out its fresh life forces and colours, perfumes and subtle nectars, that the butterflies and bees assimilate, spiritualize and make available to all beings, so we breathe out our spiritualized creative thoughts, feelings and deeds, which the Christ takes into Himself, spiritualizes further and distributes far and wide in the cosmos. In this sense, etheric breathing, nourishment, and knowledge is spiritualized further, and becomes sacred spiritual marriage and fertilization, in which our whole being is the chalice that receives and conceives the 'I' of Christ and gives it spiritual birth in the etheric world.[71]

For this reason, the given meeting with the etheric Christ led to a long and complex spiritual-scientific research. We had to form a new path to develop the required spiritual cognitive breathing, to breathe and pulse consciously together with the etheric Christ. And the required clues were found in the above-described indications of Rudolf Steiner's concerning the modern 'will of yoga' of Michael.

In this way, a spiritual breathing practice could be formed, that proved most akin to the original given experience. But from the very start of this path, we could only feel justified to actualize it, to the extent in which we could feel it in the sense of Paul's maxim, 'not "I" but Christ in me'. Since the end of the last century, it became possible to give birth to a new, spiritualized Michaelic breathing activity, and to create the bridge over the abyss that separates ordinary consciousness from the etheric world in which the etheric Christ appears. This made it possible to 'enter the Grail Castle for the second time', voluntarily, and with wakeful spiritual cognition, to investigate, individualize and recapitulate the giving of the 'I' of the Christ. This bridge could only be constructed from the substances and forces of the purest soul activity that humans can develop in this age, which is 'love in its spiritual form', as Rudolf Steiner called it in *The Philosophy of Freedom*. This bridge could be built because, as Rudolf Steiner pointed out, 'in my books *Truth and Knowledge* and *The Philosophy of Freedom*... the Pauline spirit lives... *A bridge can be built from this philosophy to the Christ Spirit*'.[72]

---

[71] In the new edition of *The New Experience of the Supersensible*, the spiritualization of breathing and the sacramental life processes will be described in greater detail.

[72] Lecture of 4 September 1917 (GA 176). My italics.

Chapter 5
The Abyss and the Event of the Threshold

The combination of the Michaelic Yoga and the Pauline method, on which the Platonic-Aristotelian essence exchange in based, forms the bridge that leads from *The Philosophy of Freedom* to the modern Christ experience. It became the starting point and foundation of the entire knowledge drama of the Second Coming. But before we describe some aspects of the knowledge drama, we must explicate its starting point. The starting point is characterized by the fact that the given meeting with the etheric Christ lifts man to the etheric body and world and offers him a seed of the 'I' of Christ. Man finds himself in this situation and event as a given grace, and the Christ provides the forces that support our etheric existence and imaginative perception, as long as the meeting lasts. But when the experience is over, we do not return to ordinary consciousness, but neither can we hold onto the given imaginative consciousness. We find ourselves in a special situation, in-between ordinary and supersensible consciousness, that we call 'the abyss and the event of the Threshold'. And this situation and event is our new spiritual homeland, in which our new spiritual existence is grounded. We understand that the spiritual world has left us wholly free to marshal our spiritual forces, to build a conscious and voluntary bridge to the Christ in the etheric world by means of modern spiritual science or to decide to return to ordinary physical consciousness in the physical world, without pursuing this possibility further.

This abyss is therefore the place through which the etheric Christ appears, speaks, and acts, in the first meeting, as a graceful gift of His new revelation; and it is the same abyss through which we must pass, to meet Him again in the voluntarily achieved second meeting, rising out of it to face Him, as He faced us in the first meeting.

> If we take the trouble to learn to think the thoughts of Spiritual Science and make the mental effort necessary for an understanding of the Cosmic secrets taught by Spiritual Science, then, out of the dark gloomy [*düster*] foundations of the Cosmic mysteries, will come forth the figure of Christ Jesus, which will draw near to us and give us the strength and force in which we

shall then live. The Christ will guide us, standing beside us as a brother, so that our hearts and souls may be strong enough to grow up to the necessary level of the tasks awaiting humanity in its further development. Let us then try to acquire Spiritual Science, not as a mere doctrine but as a language, and then wait till we can find in that language, the questions which we may venture to put to the Christ. He will answer; yes, indeed, He will answer! Plentiful indeed will be the soul-forces, the soul-strengthening, the soul-impulses, which the student will carry away with him from the grey spiritual depths through which humanity in its evolution is now passing, if he is able to receive instructions from Christ Himself; for, in the near future He will give them to those who seek.[73]

When we individualize and recapitulate the modern Christ experience through spiritual science, the spiritual being of spiritual science is felt to be, at first, a stern Guardian of the Threshold. Later, we learn that this being is Michael. His invisible being and activity stimulates us to prove to ourselves that we can prepare to cross the Threshold to meet the etheric Christ in the etheric world for the second time, in free spiritual activity. The clear distinction between the given meeting with the Christ and the meeting through the path of the knowledge drama of the Second Coming, is based on the fact that Michael firmly rejects all half-baked and premature advances, and constantly points back to the free spiritual activity of the human 'I'; he is indicating that the love of freedom—that he so loyally protects—must be gained on the earth below, and that we must come fully equipped with these forces to the Threshold to cross it in a way justified in his eyes. In other words, this means that we must freely decide to give up everything we received as a gift of grace in the first given meeting with the Christ, and freely develop our spiritual forces, in the situation at the abyss and the event on the Threshold. When man experiences this situation, he must never underestimate the power of Lucifer and Ahriman who tempt us to believe that we have developed the gracefully given forces, and that we can use

---

[73] Lecture of 6 February 1917 (GA 175). The situation and event of the Threshold is this grey and gloomy abyss, out of which the etheric Christ appears, speaks and acts, and essentially, all the contents of *The New Experience of the Supersensible* express our efforts to describe this conversation with the etheric Christ.

them to cross the Threshold, in a way that sharply contradicts the will of Michael and Christ in the present age.[74]

The given meeting with the Christ is a real supersensible experience. Therefore, its conscious investigation must come to terms with the ordeals and probations of the Threshold because the Threshold's abyss is the situation and event in which it takes place. If we are to meet the Christ again in the etheric world through the knowledge drama, we must make ourselves familiar with this abyss. The conscious way to the second meeting with the Christ must lead us through this abyss, and we must experience the abyss consciously. What unconsciously took place in the past century for all humanity, must be individualized and consciously recapitulated by the pupils of Michael since the end of the twentieth century. It is the only possible preparation for the true and healthy crossing of the Threshold. 'Before the middle of this century has passed, the Christ must be seen. But before that, all that remains of the old must be driven into nullity, the clouds must gather. The human being must find his full freedom out of nullity and the new perception must be born out of this nullity. The human being must find his whole strength out of the nothingness. It is but the desire of spiritual science to prepare him for it. This is something of which one may not say that it desires to, but that it must desire to!'[75] We must desire this most undesirable 'birth out of nullity', and the enthusiasm required to kindle in the etheric heart the flame of this courage can only be given by the etheric Christ in the present age, if we approach the mysteries of His Second Coming with the strength of Michael.

This is the above-mentioned 'grey spiritual depths through which humanity in its evolution is now passing... the dark gloomy foundations of the Cosmic mysteries', out of which the Christ appears, speaks and acts. And the fully conscious second meeting with Him is only possible if we can pass through this abyss voluntarily, and go out into the etheric world to meet Him, as He came forward to meet us in the first meeting.

---

[74] This temptation is all the stronger, the more people delude themselves about the true nature of their given visionary faculties. Such gifts are then taken over by Lucifer and Ahriman, and create real havoc in their spiritual-perceptions, which they and their numerous followers take to be true results of spiritual-scientific research.

[75] Lecture of 30 October 1920 (GA 200).

What Michael insists on most sternly is that at the Threshold of the spiritual world, man will wholly change his experience and understanding concerning the nature of cognition. Man must learn to experience that all his abstract conceptual knowledge gained on earth and stored in his brain is not only something completely external to his real being but is a major obstacle to achieve wakeful spiritual consciousness. What we know, and above all *how* we know things in the physical world, puts us to sleep at the Threshold. And we must develop this wakefulness over many years of intensive struggles with our stubborn intellectual habits, inclinations, and instincts, that we bring with us from the physical world.

Let us hold firmly to what man experiences at the abyss and event of the Threshold. He finds himself in a situation in which, on the one hand, the excarnation from the physical and etheric bodies is already accomplished, but on the other, the spiritual birth of the soul and spirit forces has not yet been fully realized. Man feels that he does not truly exist spiritually, that he dies perpetually and falls asleep on the Threshold, so long as he has not resolutely annihilated all earthly contents and forms of knowledge. Man must struggle to reach the point where he can actively *become* this nothingness and make it into the deliberately actualized nothingness of his being. Then he experiences that everything belonging to the soul life on earth becomes an unbearable burden, fettering the dormant wings of the soul and hindering their unfolding. He feels that all earthly soul contents lull him to sleep and cause him to lose his spirit light and consciousness in this darkness. He must find the strength and courage to voluntarily die to his earthly cognition before he can be born again in the light of spiritual knowledge shining from the other side of the Threshold. In other words, what takes place by itself after physical death, the liberation from the three bodies, the death of earthly consciousness and the birth of spirit consciousness, must be accomplished consciously, through our own conscious activity. This is the quintessence of the ordeal in the abyss and the event of the Threshold.

The spiritual activity developed in this abyss must therefore be based on 'a strong, determined decision of the will, to root out, to forget the memory of what we have been, in all its detail... one stands in the fullest sense of the word at the *abyss of existence* when one makes the decision in true freedom and energy of will, to blot out and forget oneself... to stand in the spiritual world as a nothing on the edge of the abyss of nothingness. This is the most shattering experience one can have; one must approach it with great confidence that the true Ego will be brought to us out of the cosmos'. This confidence is the only thing that one is allowed to carry in one's 'I' from the given Christ experience, that the true Ego—Christ's given Ego—will come to meet him 'out of the cosmos'. And only then we find out that 'this is indeed the case... out of a yet unknown world... our real Ego.... comes toward us'.

Now this is not simply a grace given to us, but rather the creation of a grace in which we are fully active, and our freedom is its determining force. 'Only now do we meet our true Ego... the perceiving of a completely new world at the edge of the abyss, the receiving of the true Ego from this world'.[76] And this means, as we shall see below, that the Ego of Christ can approach us again, a second time, because now we approached it freely and voluntarily, and what was given as pure grace in the first meeting is individualized and recapitulated in the second meeting, through the free knowledge drama of the Second Coming. Then man finds 'that abyss... between the sensory world and the spiritual world... where he is shown a kind of bridge which leads over to a completely different world, at the entrance of which lies the threshold to knowledge and to the spiritual world'.[77] And this bridge is constructed in the knowledge drama over the abyss and Michael supervises and directs this entire construction process.

The still invisible presence of Michael is felt at this stage very closely and intimately, and his greatest support is felt when he continuously rejects all our earthly soul contents and habits of knowledge. One feels his supporting will as a mighty firewall, that separates everything that man has become in earthly life from everything that he must become to cross the Threshold. But we can only truly comprehend this event if we do not merely think it abstractly with our heads and add it to the collection of intellectual anthroposophical concepts. If we merely make mental pictures of it, we certainly will not understand, let alone actualize, the crossing of the Threshold in the Age of Michael. It must become an existential spiritual disposition and instinct, that penetrates and transforms our entire being.

---

[76] Lecture of 30 August 1913 (GA 147).
[77] Lecture of 3 April 1924 (GA 270c).

In what follows, we describe some concrete examples of the meditative practice developed at this stage of the knowledge drama. We should, however, bear in mind that these are but single examples, taken out of a much greater context of many variations.

We place the following thought in the centre of our meditation. We say to ourselves: In earthly existence man gains and maintains a sustainable and substantial state of mind when he fills his consciousness with the *abiding, remembered contents and ingrained habits* of his past soul activity. Because he is positively focused on this content and these habits, which give him his solid and endurable earthly identity, he usually forgets the living soul activity and spiritual, dynamic becoming that brought it about. Or in the language of *The Philosophy of Freedom*, 'Will and feeling still fill the soul with warmth even when we live through the original event again in retrospect. Thinking all too readily leaves us cold in recollection; it is as if the life of the soul had dried out. Yet this is really nothing but the strongly marked shadow of its real nature—warm, luminous, and penetrating deeply into the phenomena of the world.'[78]

And now we must feel the reality of the corpse of thinking intensively. We must feel how our personal identity crystallizes around this memorized, habitual, dead soul content. And this leads us, by further concentration and meditation, to experience the following fact. We begin to experience that by means of the sum-total of the mental pictures that man has engraved in his soul during earthly life, he becomes a free being on earth, but has also died to the spiritual world. This is an important experience in the knowledge drama of the Second Coming at this stage, and it takes many years of practice to fully individualize and assimilate it, to *become* what it truly means. And when this experience becomes a consistent existential situation and event, we begin to experience its inversion, or *Umstülpung*, at the Threshold. We feel how our entire being is beginning to undergo this *Umstülpung*, complete turning inside out.

When this happens, we experience that at the Threshold, all existing soul contents become a heavy burden. This burden must *die* away, if man is to *live* consciously in the abyssal situation; but he must let his ordinary identity die together with it. As a

---

[78] *The Philosophy of Freedom*, Chapter 8, Author's Additions to the second edition 1918 (GA 4).

spiritual snake, he must be ready to shed his dead skin, and trust that his essential spiritual being will be resurrected alive and shining, phoenix-like, out of its corpse. Here, in this situation, his earthly identity and reality must first disappear entirely before he can be resurrected to new conscious spirit life in the stream of world becoming.

But we must find the courage—as Rudolf Steiner pointed out above—to trust the goodness of the spiritual world, and above all, to trust that not our 'I' but the power of the 'I' of Christ in us, will resurrect us on the other shore of this abyss. Only if we can fully die, can we also fully be resurrected, but this cannot be accomplished by our ordinary soul forces. Then we experience how we are rejuvenated from the expanses of the etheric world that flow towards us from the whole circumference and resurrect us out of the nothingness of the abyss. Then man can be granted the modern Pauline Christ experience: Not 'I' (in so far as this 'I' is embodied in the contents of earthly consciousness), but my Self is active, therefore I AM. This becomes our new situation and event meditation. This meeting and essence exchange between the 'I' of Christ and the human 'I', becomes thus the living centre of the knowledge drama of the Second Coming.

This experience constitutes a new ground of the groundless, selfless, self-conscious spiritual becoming at the Threshold. But only through the repeated practice of the living annihilation of all soul contents and habits, does man develop the power that gradually cracks the hardened shell of his enclosing mental egg. And it is out of this hardened enclosure that the 'wings of passage' are released in due course, carrying him over the grey and dark-gloomy abyss into the luminous spirit land in which the etheric Christ appears.

When we practice this spiritual activity, we feel how the dead forces of the Mind Soul die out, and the youthful and vibrant forces of the Consciousness Soul emerge and flourish. In the first part of the present age of the Consciousness Soul, the intellectualized Mind Soul took over and suppressed the newly emerging forces of the Consciousness Soul; as a result, man has become intellectualized and ahrimanized. But the active, creative spiritual activity, developed by means of Rudolf Steiner's *Truth and Science* and *The Philosophy of Freedom*, liberates the spiritual forces of the Consciousness Soul, and lets them grow out of their youthful spiritual sources, that have nothing in common with the old and fallen intellectualism of the fourth cultural epoch. This means the release of the soul from all physically gained elements of knowledge: abstract concepts, mental pictures, memories and above all, the deeply ingrained thought habits of our rationalistic-materialistic age. In the actual practice of the knowledge drama, this must first be accomplished, because it is the fundamental condition for gaining first-hand supersensible knowledge.[79]

To draw near to the abyss of the Threshold in full consciousness, man must, above all, overcome the two great 'knowledge enemies' of our ahrimanic age: first, the belief in a physical or spiritually given and objective 'Reality' that is directly accessible to us without our creative cognitive efforts and that can be passively perceived and acquired; and second, the belief that 'Truth' can be represented as a mental picture, and be taken hold of and privatized as an enduring mental possession in the personal collection of 'my own truths'. For the pupil of anthroposophical spiritual science this becomes an even greater challenge, because he carries in his mental reservoir a rich treasure of knowledge, composed of many concepts and representations, objectively given in the books and institutions created by spiritual science a century ago.

The given content of anthroposophy makes it possible to remember it in ordinary consciousness, and we must have this dead spiritual skeleton for our mental support in our time. But it should be used only as an aid to memory, to fire our creative spiritual activity again and again; otherwise, it easily becomes the heavy and passive content of a traditionally transmitted belief system, that paralyzes real spiritual activity and makes the Mind Soul of the Middle Ages dominant over the Consciousness Soul. This becomes detrimental for any effort to create living anthroposophy in the physical world, because it totally blocks the real path to the spiritual world.

------

[79] 'Just as the ego in ordinary life feels independent of its own recollections, so our newly-found ego feels itself independent of our former ego. It feels that it belongs to a world of purely spiritual beings. And as this experience—a real experience: no mere theory—comes to us, so we understand the real nature of what we have formerly considered to be our self. It presents itself as a web of recollections, produced by the physical, the elemental and the astral bodies in the same way as an image is produced by a mirror... The web of recollection which we now regard as our former ego may be called the "ego-body" or "thought-body".' (*A Road to Self-Knowledge*, sixth meditation, GA 16.)

On the spiritual path it becomes a heavy burden, the more man approaches the threshold of spiritual reality.

One observes how many souls are continuously tempted in this regard, and refuse to give it up, clinging to what they know through their earthly intellect *about* the spiritual worlds, placing this dead content in the place of the *real* spiritual world, and totally blocking their path. They tenaciously hold on to the dead content of their concepts and thoughts habits when the Guardian of the Threshold requires us to abolish them and these souls also refuse rather aggressively his advice to actively annihilate all physical and intellectual contents of earthly consciousness. The tragic fate of these souls ever since the beginning of the last century, is caused, as Rudolf Steiner said, because 'in reality, the most fatal thing of all for a true occultist is to long to penetrate into spiritual science without desiring at the same time to do so differently than in the case of knowledge concerning the physical world.'[80]

This fatal trap so common in the present age of intellectualism, must be thoroughly overcome on the Threshold, and before this is fully accomplished, there is no possibility of gaining true spiritual scientific knowledge. Nor can *The Philosophy of Freedom* become the foundation of the knowledge drama of the Second Coming before this is accomplished, because the spiritual meaning of 'freedom' is revealed only then. 'It is not possible to acquire a knowledge of the spiritual world in this [ordinary intellectual] way. On the contrary, the books dealing with the spiritual world should stimulate our inner activity anew each time we read them; they should each time bring new life and movement into our inner forces... freedom is something that can be held fast only through constantly arising anew. Freedom is something that a human being must acquire anew at each moment, and as a matter of fact he can really acquire it only *when there arises in his soul at each moment a trace of his meeting the spiritual world*. Look it up in my book *The Philosophy of Freedom*.'[81] This is what it takes to enter in full consciousness into the abyss and event of the Threshold, that separates the first, given meeting with the Christ, from the second, freely gained meeting.

A properly developing spiritual-scientific praxis, though it necessarily begins with the study of the given anthroposophical

---

[80] Lecture of 29 May 1915 (GA 162).
[81] Ibid. My italics.

matter in the physical world, must guide the pupil from the very first step to experience the immense difference, indeed, the full reversal, between the finished contents of knowledge and the dynamic *creative activity* that creates spiritual knowledge. That is, it must transform the passive assimilation of represented anthroposophical contents into the experiential and experimental *experience* of the ways in which true supersensible knowledge comes about, and then is killed again and again in ordinary consciousness, and how it must be resurrected repeatedly from this grave. Such an experiential practice is the necessary preparation for the knowledge drama of the Second Coming, and it alone can bring to full consciousness the modern Christ experience in its complex form.

This becomes an embodied, existential experience of life, a new spiritual habit, because of the meditations developed to address the requirements of the Threshold's abyss and event. In this way, we accomplish consciously what was first offered as a gift of grace in the given Christ experience. As we described in Chapter 4 of *The New Experience of the Supersensible*, in the given meeting, man already lives and weaves in the abyss opened through a separation of the soul forces, which extends also to the bodily sheaths and forces. This separation expresses itself, to begin with, in the loosening of the unconscious, instinctive connection between thinking and sense-perception. In this event, the mental picture, by means of which we represent the external world when we combine our thinking with our sense-perceptions, falls apart. This means that there is a certain disintegration of the objective world picture and the normal self-centred identity connected with it, which must be brought to full consciousness if it is to become a source of blessing to man's development and not the cause of mental disorientation and confusion.

To bring this aspect of the Threshold to consciousness, we created the following meditative practice, that was experienced as particularity fruitful in this situation. It was developed according to Rudolf Steiner's indication in his seminal book, *The Riddles of the Soul*, in which he described the significance of the formation of what he called 'Grenz Vorstellungen' or 'representations that arise at the boundary'. He writes that these representations portray unthinkable and unrepresentable spiritual realities, but that their spiritual value lies not in what they represent, but in the *intensity of feeling* that they cause to arise in the soul. To create this intensity is the aim of their formation, and our experience has proved that this intensity, once it is generated, creates unique soul forces, by means of which one can live and weave in the abyss with growing consciousness.

What this meditative experience of boundary representations teaches us is how to let all represented contents of thinking die out in the abyss, and yet sustain one's self-consciousness at the Threshold, fully awake, without attachment to any earthly contents.[82] To achieve this, during many years, I repeatedly placed in the centre of my soul Rudolf Steiner's exactly delimited point of departure of all free and fully conscious human knowledge. This point of departure portrays how the world would appear if we merely gazed at it without any thinking. For this purpose, among others, it proved fruitful to create and apply boundary representations from Rudolf Steiner's doctoral dissertation, *Truth and Science*. For example, we find there the typical boundary representation of the 'directly given' external world, as it would appear if we removed from it all the results of thinking. Working with this boundary representation leads man to the abyss in a very secure and grounded manner. Let us describe this practice more closely.

In our meditation, we first build up, step by step, the human constitution in the physical world and its world picture. We experience how during earthly life, the physical, etheric, astral and Ego members of our being, are integrated unconsciously, without our knowledge, and how their combined activity create a solid picture of a fixed external world. This meditation brings about a differentiated experience of the contribution of each body and member to the formation of earthly consciousness. Schematically, this can be represented as follows.

1. The senses of the physical body are responsible for the fact that the world picture does not constantly flit past us but is grasped and held firmly by the physical body.
2. The etheric body, united with the physical, brings it about that all sense-perceptions, as well as the inner events of the soul life, are

---

[82] This is done in the present context of the abyssal situation and event, in which we must facilitate a secure and reliable crossing of the Threshold. It must be emphasized that the repeated practice of the basic meditative exercises of *Knowledge of the Higher Worlds* and *Occult Science* form the foundation of the knowledge drama, as described in the new edition of *The New Experience of the Supersensible*.

experienced as basically *connected* with one another and form *one* world picture.

3. The astral body brings into this pre-established unity the awareness of *differentiated* details, that make it saturated with abiding sensory content.

4. The Ego distinguishes, relates, and determines this manifold but thoroughly united world picture and carries it in its power of memory as its own possession, as an inwardly sustained and condensed sense of solid self-conscious identity.

Now we actively suppress one by one the connecting forces of the physical, etheric, astral bodies and the Ego, and generate the 'directly given' picture of the world, described by Rudolf Steiner in *Truth and Science*, in this way:

This directly given picture is what,

1. flits past us;
2. disconnected;
3. undifferentiated.
4. Nothing appears distinguished from, related to, or determined by, anything else.[83]

The goal of this exercise is to take apart and annul, voluntarily, all the unconscious connecting and synthesizing forces that determine the form and contents of ordinary consciousness. *And this conscious taking apart of the unconscious formative forces of ordinary cognition, is the formation process of fully conscious spiritual cognition.* The nearer we draw to the Threshold, 'the grey and gloomy spirit abyss' out of which the etheric Christ appears, this coherent and solid sense of a separate 'I' and its physical world picture increasingly disintegrates and falls apart. The seed-centre of the soul and spirit strives to be experienced wholly free from everything that in one way or another has been gathered in the world of ordinary sense-and-thought life. The meditation on the boundary representation of the given world picture and its disintegration, prepares the soul to experience this abyss in full consciousness. It proved its usefulness precisely in this regard because it established voluntarily what takes place as a given

---

[83] *Truth and Science* (GA 3). Numeration added for clarity. This meditation is greatly enhanced due to the natural evolutionary separation of the etheric body from the physical heart and the transformation of the whole human constitution that it brings about, as described in Chapter 3 of *The New Experience of the Supersensible*, 'The Evolution of Freedom'.

event in the meeting with the Christ in the modern Christ experience, and alone can bring to full consciousness the situation of the abyss and the event of the Threshold.

With the new cognitive forces, gained in the above-described meditative exercise, we return to *Riddles of the Soul* and concentrate them on this precise point. 'The soul must be familiar with the inner process that combines representation with sense-perception; so familiar that *it can hold at arm's length* the influx of the sense-perceptions themselves (or of their echoes in after-experience) into the act of representing.' This 'holding at arm's length of the influx of sense-perceptions' can be accomplished very precisely, with the cognitive faculties developed previously, because we trained ourselves in separating thinking from perception. 'This keeping at bay of the formation of sensory representations can only be achieved if one has detected the way in which the *activity* of representing occurs.' Representation occurs when we combine our thoughts in an unconscious, instinctive manner, with sense-perceptions.

When we consciously cancel this unconscious combination, as we did above, we free the soul forces from the grip of sensory representation. At this moment, they revert to their original spiritual function, which is imaginative perception. As Rudolf Steiner says, 'not until then is one in a position to *combine one's spiritual organs with the act itself* and thereby to receive perceptions of spiritual reality'. The liberated imaginative force, usually *Herabgelähmt* or paralyzed by sense-perception, unites with the spiritual organs, and perceives the spiritual reality behind ordinary perception and thinking alike, as we showed also in *Cognitive Yoga*. 'Thus, the act of representing is impregnated from quite another side than in the case of sense-perception'. But how do we accomplish, in spiritual practice, this '*holding at arm's length* the influx of the sense-impressions... into the act of representing'? Above, we pointed out what takes place in the soul when we actualize, repeatedly, the boundary representation of the 'directly given' picture described in *Truth and Knowledge*. Let us now traverse this way again and zoom in to describe some of its concrete features.

In the meditative practice, this 'directly given' boundary representation annihilates itself in its very coming-into-being; it can therefore be transformed into a unique cognitive faculty that can lift to full self-consciousness the situation at the abyss and the event of the Threshold, in which ordinary consciousness dies out. The death of ordinary thinking and representing in the nothingness of this abyss becomes—during this practice—the birth of higher and infinitely more vital consciousness. What we discover is that this boundary representation is transformed in the meditation into an *inverse* soul space and force, experienced as an actively produced *non-relation* between thinking and sense-perception. This active non-relation is a productive spiritual force; it *gives up* the ground structure and formative forces that form, consolidate and preserve ordinary consciousness. In other words: it releases the formative forces of ordinary consciousness from the brain and senses and lifts them up to the etheric brain.

This release and lifting up causes a complete metamorphosis of the formative forces of cognition. We experience their liberation and resurrection from the ahrimanic grave of the brain. We are present, when we do this, in the sacred birth moment of imaginative cognition out of ordinary cognition, of the Imaginative Soul out of the Consciousness Soul. We experience how the higher spiritual forces get hold of the formative forces of ordinary cognition and transform them into the formative forces of imaginative cognition. This transformation and spiritualization of the physical, brain-bound etheric formative forces, that shape, consolidate and preserve ordinary consciousness, into the etheric formative forces of imaginative consciousness, is the crucial transformation that takes place in this abyss and event at the Threshold. One enters the abyss by losing earthly consciousness altogether and emerges from it with the first self-conscious faculties of the new imaginative cognition.

Let us determine again how ordinary consciousness comes into existence. It comes into existence when the 'I' forms, by means of the etheric forces bound to the physical body and brain, the constant synthesis of thinking and sense-perception. This synthesis results in the production of memorable mental pictures, or representations. The spiritual activity of giving up and inverting this synthetic activity is the etheric foundation of the knowledge drama of the Second Coming. This must be firmly grasped in our spiritual praxis, not as a mere idea, but as a spiritual act. The individuation of the 'I' in the physical world occurs through the repeated formation of representations, in the synthetic activity of each act of gaining ordinary knowledge.

When man reflects on these fixed mental results *after* this activity is over, he perceives only its dead corpses, the remembered mental

finished results of this activity, all while the living activity itself
is long past. He has then within his waking consciousness only
the dying, devitalized picture-shadow and corpse of its finished
result.[84] Now this is a decisive moment that must be grasped in all
exactitude: spiritually seen, every coming to rest of soul-and-spirit
activity creates a fixed and permanent mental sedimentation, which
can later be remembered in consciousness as a left-over corpse of
a living event, bound to past time. A closer look at this coming to
rest in the grave of previous spiritual activity reveals a threefold
devitalizing structure. 1. it *contracts*, and thereby, 2. *condenses*, and
finally, 3. *suppresses* the living life-stream, that flows from the future
reservoir of potential life forces; it creates in its vacant, negative
shadow-place—where the future time stream was dammed, suppressed, and annihilated—an abiding, reversed and isolated dead
picture, a mere representation of what was living spiritual reality.

On the surface of this dense and opaque mirror, created by the
synthesized brain-bound products of its former living activity,
the real 'I' reflects and pictures *itself* and thus makes itself into a
self-conscious being.[85] In this way, it stamps a preservable imprint
of its unseen spiritual being and, together with the growing treasures of engraved and fixed, privatized and reversed, world-corpse
pictures, gains a stronger hold of itself as a self-centred self; it separates itself from the spiritual world, and firmly incarnates in the
physical body and world.

Now at this stage we make a remarkable discovery concerning
the relation between the activity of the real spiritual 'I' and the formation of its representations and memories. We discover that the
real 'I', while it busily multiplies the represented treasures of ordinary consciousness through external sense-perception and intellectual reflection, *in spiritual reality* is not interested at all in increas-
ing their quantity. While it produces the representations in daily
cognition and amalgamates the fixed and remembered intellectual
results of these past acts of knowledge, unconsciously (for our daily
consciousness) the real 'I' is constantly inverting this process. In
the 'night consciousness' (in which the real 'I' lives also during the
day), that prevails one level below the brain-bound, wakeful, daily

---

[84] This process is described also in the lecture of 14 December 1915
(GA 157a).
[85] See lecture of 11 April 1914 (GA 153).

consciousness, in which the production of representations occurs, it constantly unbuttons this process.

We discover—when we view this process from *both sides* of the Threshold—that the real 'I' is not at all as greedy as the ordinary 'I' is; it is rather much more interested in enhancing the inner energy and quality of the power of spiritual activity and production and uses the constant night-inversion of ordinary consciousness for this purpose. Now we know that 'what man stores up in his memory is a curtain woven across the spiritual reality... a far greater striving must arise for a ceaseless activity and an active participation in things, and the tendency to say, "We have understood this, now we can carry it about with us through life" must disappear.'[86] And indeed, it disappears entirely, when the above-described *Umstülpung* process between ordinary and suppressible cognition is actualized and perceived.

This hidden supersensible relation can be lifted to imaginative cognition through practicing an inversion of the synthetic activity of ordinary knowledge. This happens after we have succeeded in 'holding at arm's length the influx of the sense-perceptions into the act of representing', according to *Riddles of the Soul*. We cancel and give up the automatic brain-bound synthesis of thinking and sense-perception and halt the creation of the next mental picture. In the moment in which this synthetic brain-bound activity is annulled, and the abyss opens, the situation and event of the Threshold, described above, surfaces. Our ordinary consciousness is annihilated as well because it is grounded, supported, and nourished by the continuous steam of despiritualized and devitalized sense-perceptions and representations. But with it our ordinary self-consciousness also dies out because the ordinary perception of our self and the picture of the physical world are also only a mental representation, reflected by the dead opaque mirror of the physical brain. This moment becomes an archetypal situation at the abyss and event of the Threshold; and we repeat this meditative practice whenever we wish to restart the knowledge drama, in order to meet voluntarily the Christ, Michael and Anthroposophia in the etheric world.

In this moment, when the sunset of our ordinary consciousness sinks into the nocturnal darkness of the abyss below, lightning

---

[86] Lecture of 29 May 1915 (GA 162).

strikes from above, from the other side of the Threshold, illuminating the spiritual activity of the real 'I'. The lightning also reveals the fact that beneath the threshold of ordinary consciousness, that is, in supersensible reality, the real 'I' unceasingly inverts and thereby enlivens the threefold mental devitalization process of ordinary consciousness. That is, we discover that the night process takes place parallel to the day process, and that when we acquire ordinary knowledge by representing in the physical world, by contrast, in the supersensible world, the real 'I' is constantly inverting this process.

We see how the 'night' 'I', 1. *unblocks* the suppressed, future time and life-stream, and thereby, 2. *dissolves* the dead past mental condensations, and finally, 3. *releases* the blocking, killing, and suppressing congestion. In this flashing light that lights up the supersensible night, we see our real 'I' as it works, simultaneously, *from both sides of the Threshold,* regulating the two opposite processes, from the middle sphere between day and night; as the physical creation of ordinary consciousness takes place in the brain, its inverting happens in the etheric brain, and the real 'I' uses the etheric heart to regulate and coordinate the two streams of life and time. We see that when the real 'I' annihilates, enlivens, and resurrects the formative forces of representation, it goes unhindered *backwards from the future to the past* through the mental pictures that resulted from its brain-bound acts of knowledge. It makes them light-filled and transparent through this hidden, invisible night inverting activity, and it reveals how it strengthens and increases its living lighting power through this inversion. The more conscious and active our self-conscious spiritual activity becomes, the more the night process lights up in imaginative cognition; the more we transform thinking into the pure stream of future oriented will, into self-accelerating dynamical movement, and stop and cancel the creations of new mental pictures, the more the real 'I' becomes visible in the etheric world.

And the moment comes in which both sides and activities of the real 'I', in the 'day' and 'night', hidden behind each act of physical knowledge, merge together, and when this happens, the first outlines of the bridge over the abyss of the Threshold become visible. Because we gained the ability to raise this hidden night work into fuller and fuller spiritual consciousness and exact imaginative perception and cognition, we can exactly delimit where and when the foundation of the bridge of spiritual memory and continuation of consciousness is to be grounded in the knowledge drama of the Second Coming.[87]

Now, when this happens, we observe how the real 'I' grows and increases its potency and substance as an active spiritual being, by means of its ability to energize itself while streaming backward in the stream of future time; what otherwise happens only in deep unconsciousness in sleep and after death, comes to conscious spiritual light and knowledge when the 'I' annihilates, transforms, enlivens and resurrects its dead mental corpses and representations; thus it unites itself increasingly with the cosmic forces of new, resurrected life, that flow *towards* it *through* every freed and resurrected, etherized, light-giving and shining *Imagination*. Then each physical representation is revealed in its true essence, as the dead corpse of pre-earthly life, that dies in the brain-grave of the modern ahrimanic intellect; it disappears in the abyss that opens up when the 'soul's grave shakes and fissures' in the spiritual earthquake that shakes the etheric world in the second Mystery of Golgotha; but from the selfsame abyss it emerges again, revealing how its new life rises from the grave, shining, life-giving, resurrected and transfigured.

This is the resurrected 'phantom' of the soul and the thought body, the resurrected etheric body and new imaginative cognition. The light of resurrection shines through the spiritual sunrise of each spiritualized representation when the resurrected phantom of thinking and sense-perception becomes the living body of imagination. We see in all clarity, in detail and precision, how each dead mental picture is resurrected as an Imaginative picture, when the etheric formative forces of the brain-bound intellect are transformed in the etheric brain and heart into the resurrected etheric formative forces of the new, Christ-given, imaginative cognition. One becomes aware, in deepest devotion and reverence, that one witnesses, as a creative participant, the miraculous birth situation and event of the resurrected and spiritualized forces of the Consciousness Soul, radiating forth with the spirit light of the Imaginative Soul.

---

[87] As we show in Chapter 5 of *The New Experience of the Supersensible*, this process constitutes the formation of the first, cognitive-etheric layer of the bridge, from head to heart.

It is a new, future-orientated memory, a will-like imaginative pro-vision of the true spiritual being of the 'I', the coming Spirit Self; this imaginative perception of future life after death constitutes the inversion and resurrection of the old Platonic notion of knowledge as remembrance of the life before birth. We begin to see spiritually in the present 'the shape of things to come', as the old Platonists saw the shadow images of the dying spirit light of the past, we can now *see* the living future, the incoming spiritual stream of becoming.

In modern times, as Rudolf Steiner repeatedly emphasized, when the pre-earthly life of cosmic thinking becomes the dead corpse of physical thinking, buried in the brain-grave of modern civilization, it is the foremost task of spiritual science to unite with the etheric Christ and resurrect it out of this grave; to actualize the future imaginative seeing, and resurrect the wholly exhausted pre-earthly life of the past, in the living present. In this way, the Christ-given 'I' begins to dwell in the human 'I'. With the future time stream, it constantly resurrects the past, unites day and night, life and death, sleep and waking, and makes of the earthly and spiritual selves one true Self; it unites physical self-consciousness with spiritual consciousness to form a fully 'bridged' spiritual self-consciousness that lives and works in both worlds, with full consciousness and knowledge of the physical life while in the spiritual world, and of the spiritual world while living in the physical world.

In this Prelude we can only indicate briefly what is described in detail in Chapter 5 of *The New Experience of the Supersensible*. An indication of this can be given if we observe this process from another point of view.

A closer investigation of the act of knowledge in its *totality*, from both sides of the Threshold, reveals that whenever the 'I' resurrects and passes on its way backward from the future to the past through a mental picture, it lights up and radiates with an intense illumination it did not have before. Why does the 'I', as a real spirit being, light up in this passing-through? Because *this backward passing-through is a self-recollection—or self-remembering—of the real 'I' to itself from the vast periphery of its dismembered and scattered universal existence*. While in ordinary consciousness the results of the acts of knowledge crystallize into finished mental forms, below the threshold of this consciousness the real 'I' inverts this crystallization constantly, spiritualizes and extracts the spirit essence from each dying mental picture; but in each and every brain-bound and engraved representation, feeling, desire and will impulse, the dismembered fragments of the universal spirit of the spiritual 'I' are buried, and through the resurrection of each and every soul fragment, dead self-consciousness is also resurrected, as an individualized Dionysus and Osiris. Ordinary self-consciousness meets and unites itself with its spiritual self, which, unhindered by man's representations, comes to meet it through every sense-perception. But every representation leaves an enduring dead and darkening *trace* in the living light of man and the world. It is this opaque shadowy trace-residue that originally divides the universal whole human-world being into seemingly two wholly disconnected, unrecognized halves: into an inner thinking, feeling, willing 'self' and an externally perceived 'world'. Now the two halves of our whole human-world 'I' meet each other and merge for the first time in full self-consciousness, creating a wholly new state of supersensible, imaginative, self-consciousness, which is Christ's gift to humanity, given through Michael, in the age of the Consciousness Soul.

This primordial world-self wholeness would remain unconscious to itself if it could not come to meet itself first as a divided contradiction, made of two disconnected halves of inner self *and* external world; it is this separation alone that can consolidate and ignite a separate state of self-consciousness in the forming of each devitalized mental picture. But now the time for turning of Platonism on its head has fully commenced. This happens when *the power of separation and individuation itself is resurrected*. The power used to separate the human being from the world is transformed, through Christ's etheric appearance, words and deeds, into the very power that connects man in full self-consciousness with the cosmos. It is thanks to Rudolf Steiner's redemptive deed, that the self-conscious cognitive forces of pure thinking and sense-perception, generated in the *earthly* act of knowledge, can become an eternal power of the individualized, Christ-given 'I' of each person. Cognition has been resurrected and consecrated in this 'spiritual communion of humanity', when Rudolf Steiner actualized it for the first time in human evolution. 'What I wrote in 1888 in the second volume of my edition of Goethe's scientific writings is permeated with such views: When this thinking of the idea grows strong enough, then it merges with the fundamental existence of the world; what is at work without enters into the spirit of man: he becomes one with objective reality at its highest potency. *Becoming aware of the idea within reality is the true communion of man'.*[88]

Exactly a century later, in the 1980s and 1990s, one could individualize this sacred communion, thanks to the power flowing from the 'I' of the etheric Christ. This takes place, as we shall see below, in the knowledge drama of the Second Coming, when the ordinary process of cognition is consciously inverted and redirected to dissolve and enliven the dying and darkening residues of ordinary consciousness that enabled its coming into being in the first place. Then these future orientated, inverted cognitive forces allow the wholeness of the real spiritual 'I' to come together, recollected, and remembered, in an enhanced, rhythmical human-world, world-human breathing of supersensible knowledge.

This, therefore, is the reason why, when the 'I' transforms and resurrects each dying-darkening mental picture into a livingly shining imagination, it lights up stronger than before. It is the spiritual power of the Green Snake, pictured in Goethe's fairy tale as *The Green Snake and the Beautiful Lily*, that gathers and assimilates the scattered fragments of gold—the remnants of the old forces of Michael's cosmic intelligence that fell from the sun—from earthly rocks and crevices. While it takes them in and resurrects them by means of the power of the *new* earthly-human sun, its inner transparent brilliance grows stronger and brighter. With every assimilated and resurrected dead representation, the dynamic unrepresented force-nature of the Green Snake—which is the real 'I'—warms and lights up, the more it gathers in its scattered dismembered universal being from the periphery of sense-perception. In this manner the real 'I' forms the new etheric body that bridges the abyss of the Threshold. The act of knowledge perceived thus *from both sides of the Threshold*, means the liberation and resurrection of the sense- and brain-bound, dead and frozen formative forces of ordinary cognition. But in these ahrimanized formative forces the universal human-world 'I'—like the primeval Dionysus and Osiris—is torn to pieces, dismembered, scattered, and buried; therefore, when these are spiritualized and gathered by the new Isis, as we shall see below, to the new sun-heart of living wholeness, it is the 'I' itself that experiences itself resurrected into the full future self-consciousness of its world-human nature.

---

[88] *The Story of My Life*, Chapter 10 (GA 28).

Now this observation can be described also from another point of view. When the real 'I' carries out this work of resurrection with the forces of ordinary consciousness that create the mental picture, it penetrates and transforms the mirror of memory embedded in the devitalized part of the etheric body. This transformation has two related aspects. On the one hand, it grasps the formerly living part of the etheric body, which is continuously deadened by the consolidation of every new memorized representation and resurrects it to new life. It is a deed of resurrection, as we showed above. When it lives and weaves in this resurrected part, the 'I' spiritualizes thinking. On the other hand, because the 'I' assimilated and resurrected the death forces inherent in the mental picture, and took death into its living heart, it also kills part of the still living etheric body. And it is through this consciously killed part that the 'I' achieves conscious modern imaginative cognition. Yet the spiritualization of thinking and development of imagination happens in one and the same act. The resurrection of the dying part of the etheric body kills part of the living etheric body, and vice versa: the killing of the living part resurrects the dying part of the etheric body. This is the true meaning of 'the assimilation of death into life' that constitutes the foundation of esoteric Christianity and the 'Pauline method', and the central pillar of the knowledge drama of the Second Coming.

Now, in ordinary life, part of the etheric body is *unconsciously* killed in each new act of earthly cognition and serves the consolidation of daily waking consciousness. It is now *consciously resurrected*. The other part of the etheric body remains untouched in the killing caused by ordinary cognition. It remains deeply unconscious during ordinary life. It only becomes conscious through the resurrection of the dead part. When the living part of the etheric body offers its life to the dead part in order to resurrect it, it is *consciously killed*. At the place and stream of time where the resurrected dead life and the killed living life meet, cross, invert and exchange their essences in and through each other, something wholly new is created in human self-consciousness: a fully conscious *and* living mental-picturing faculty comes into being, that is, a fully thought-permeated, inspired, *Imagination*. In this unique and sacred place of time in which both spiritualized thinking, resurrected from the grave of ordinary thinking, and the faculty of Imagination, born out of the consciously killed etheric forces, become one cognitive faculty.

This new faculty is begotten out of the living annihilation and resurrection of the forces of death that operate in the physical basis of the Consciousness Soul. *This is the original birth event of the Imaginative soul out of the Consciousness Soul in the etheric heart.* This event is the essential result of the spiritualization of cognition in the abyss and event of the Threshold. The conscious resurrection of the death forces that create the mental picture in ordinary consciousness is, in reality, a spiritualized soul and heart birth—the birth of an immortal state of self-consciousness inside the grey-gloomy abyss of the grave of modern intellectualism and materialism, out of which 'supersensible knowledge must be resurrected because with it the knowledge of Christ Jesus will be resurrected out of this grave'.[89] This birth occurs in a unique space and stream of time which is—at the 'same' ever self-dividing, ever self-reuniting time—the interchangeable birth and death place of earthly and supersensible cognitions, transformed *inside* and *through* the other. And in this intimate essence exchange of death into life and life into death 'as a chemical combination'[90], *in this living death process of Death*, completed in the etheric heart, Christ's etheric death and resurrection in the second Mystery of Golgotha is individualized and recapitulated. Death itself is resurrected, and the foundation is created for the mutual interweaving of spiritualized thinking and imaginative perception, which constitutes the true nature of the Imaginative, Inspirative and Intuitive Souls, described in detail in *The New Experience of the Supersensible*.

For ordinary consciousness this delicate and subtle cognitive process remains unconscious. Through the knowledge drama of the Second Coming, it is lifted to full consciousness. In ordinary cognition this moment is hidden and suppressed precisely behind the formation and crystallization process of every mental picture. That this picture *rises up* and becomes fully conscious in ordinary daily cognition is due to the fact that the process described above simultaneously *sinks down* below the threshold of daily consciousness at the same *split moment* of time. The conscious spiritualization and resurrection of the act of knowledge, described here, brings the *whole* event before the inner eye: the simultaneous rising up of the

---

[89] Lecture of 2 April 1920 (GA 198).
[90] Lecture of 3 April 1915 (GA 161) and see also lecture of 22 August 1924 (GA 243).

reality-drained mental picture, and the sinking down of the reality-saturated life element, and the moment of the mutual crossing and inverting of their paths.

This process is the *Umstülpung* of the process by means of which self-consciousness is formed in the Consciousness Soul age, described by Rudolf Steiner in the following words: 'The past [thoughts] throwing its shadows, the future [forces of will] fraught with the germs of a new reality meet in the human being. And their meeting constitutes the human life of the present time', which constitutes 'the life of free human self-consciousness in the epoch of the Consciousness Soul.'[91] When this constitution is spiritualized as we show here, the formation of supersensible cognition, expected from us by the spiritual guidance of man and humanity, is actualized in the present Age of Michael. This process is described in the above-cited passage from *Riddles of the Soul* as follows: 'The conceptual life does not really get lost but carries on its existence, separated from the region of consciousness, in the unconscious spheres of the soul. And there it will be found again by spiritual organs.'

The first living place of time where the suppressed life of the mental pictures is found by the spiritual activity of the Imaginative Soul is the above-indicated moment of the twilight. In this event, the sinking down of the inner night sun and the rising of the external day sun, meet on the Threshold in-between day and night—on the newly formed imaginative horizon of consciousness. In ordinary consciousness, the daily sunrise overwhelms the inner sun of the night and takes its place. The holding fast of this *time difference* between the spiritual sunset and sunrise at the singular moment, hidden behind every twinkling of an eye, enables us to invert this process and investigate its future-backwards flow. This means to liberate man's flowing etheric body from its ahrimanic bondage to representation formation, and to open wide the time difference between night and day, sleeping and awakening, life and death, in a singular moment of fully awakened imaginative consciousness.

Instead of letting thinking and sense-perception devitalize each other in the forming of the brain- and sense-bound mental pictures, feelings, desires and will impulses, we let them flow freely *through* each other and be inverted *into* each other. Resurrected thinking thus

---

[91] *Leading Thoughts*, 'What is the Earth in reality in the Microcosmos?' (GA 26).

reaches to the living origin of imaginative perception, and imaginative perception reaches as far as the original source of spiritual thinking. Beyond their crossing point midway, in the etheric heart, they are both gradually inverted, at once keeping, transforming, and giving up their original identity in an essence exchange inside each other's opposite stream. When resurrected thinking grasps the origin of imaginative perception it becomes a fully actualized and substantial imaginative cognition; and when imaginative perception penetrates to the source of spiritual thinking it becomes, as perception, actualized and substantial, inspirative perception. In the essence exchange of spiritualized thinking and imaginative perception, thinking is perceived through imaginative perception, and imaginative perception is thought through spiritualized thinking. The first, the spiritualized thinking, *inspires* the second, and the second, imaginative perception, *imagines* the first. Thus, based on the activity of the Imaginative Soul, the inwardly saturated, Inspirative Soul is created, on which the higher, Intuitive Soul is formed. Let us briefly describe this cognitive transformation, developed in detail in Chapter 5 of *The New Experience of the Supersensible*.

During the spiritualization of the ordinary act of knowledge and its mental-picture creations, the forces are prepared that can lead to the emptying of the soul of its ordinary contents and forces. As we pointed out above, such an active voluntary emptying is a necessary precondition for self-conscious spiritual life and existence at the abyss situation and event of the Threshold. The deeper levels of the modern Christ experience are discovered only when we realize that His etheric form crystallizes in the etheric world from the 'grey-gloomy spirit abyss' of the *astral* world. This means that if we seek to penetrate to the deeper reality of the process of Christ's appearance, we must investigate the *becoming* process of this appearance and not only its finished outward etheric form. To investigate properly the etheric appearance with the research methods of modern spiritual science, we have first to spiritualize our initial imaginative perception and purify it from its external as well as internal, personal, and accidental characteristics. This is achieved to a large extent by means of the spiritualization of the act of knowledge described above and the developing of the Inspirative Soul. But the imaginative and inspired soul faculties must be developed one step further if we wish to investigate in detail the actual process through which this etheric appearance in the astral world is taking place. We must, therefore, develop the force that is able to experience and comprehend the real nature of the astral world in which this appearance takes place.

This cognitive force is developed in the knowledge drama in the following way. After we have brought it to the point described above, in which spiritualized thinking and imaginative perception meet, cross, and exchange their essences, instead of allowing them to flow in and through each other and complete each other, *we hold them fast at the point of their crossing*. We stop their accelerating movement and arbitrarily suppress their inversion into each other. We hold them at the moment when both cancel each other, before they let each other be born again in and through each other. Here we have the tiny etheric space of living time, the needle's eye, that we must gradually enlarge through the continuous inward empty-ing of its past *and* future substance. We must bring them to a stand-still and thus separate the living flow of the two streams of time from each other, at the point of their mutual inversion, in which they always momentarily annihilate and immediately enliven themselves again. We must make this ever-present, unconscious annihilation activity into a fully self-conscious self-annihilation process, in order *to overcome inwardly the substantial etheric reality of the streams of past and future time*. In this way we invert, open, and penetrate the inner structure of the 'stream of time's annihilation', the destruction process of time, and individualize it. This means to enact and realize time's inner nullity through our own soul forces and then, carrying its emptying further beyond its null point, to actualize and expand its negative time space, and ground it in ever expanding soul emptiness.[92]

This means to individuate and cross entirely the River of Lethe, the stream of time's annihilation, drink consciously the draught that causes the forgetting of all contents and events related to time and reach the timeless astral soul shore on the other side of time. *A central task of the knowledge drama of the Second Coming is to make this exit out of, and back into time, into an ever wakeful, secure, and remem-bered* bridge. We must develop this capacity, to conduct the spiritu-al-scientific research of the becoming and appearance processes of

---

[92] This is achieved through the meditative exercises given in *Occult Science* for the development of the faculties of Imagination, Inspiration and Intu-ition, described in *The New Experience of the Supersensible*.

the visible etheric body of the Christ in the soul world. As shown in Chapter 4 of *The New Experience of the Supersensible*, the etheric body of the Christ that we see becomes visible in the continuous process of etheric death and rebirth in the human etheric body. And the place in which this appearance can be brought to the light of the new intuited and inspired imaginative cognition, is the soul's experience of emptiness in the astral world, into which man enters the moment he crosses the River of Time's annihilation.

When this bridge is firmly established, it can make possible the free entry into the realm of the appearance of Christ in the astral world in His Second Coming. Then empirical supersensible research can investigate the different aspects of Christ's appearance, words, and deeds, in a way that, both methodically and experientially, fulfils the justified cognitive and scientific requirements of the present modern age. That is, it can be anchored safely in the formative cognitive forces of the Consciousness Soul, that are systematically transformed and spiritualized into the Imaginative, Inspired, and Intuitive Souls. When this threefold soul transformation is achieved, not only further differentiated and detailed knowledge of Christ's etheric appearance, words and deeds is available to supersensible research, but, through the manifold methodical ramifications and applications of modern spiritual science, it can also serve other areas of spiritual investigation in nature and in history.

Chapter 6
The Knowledge Drama of the Second Coming

The goal of the knowledge drama of the Second Coming is to create the spiritual faculties required to individualize and recapitulate the given meeting with the Christ and lead to the second, freely created meeting. This is also the creation of the bridge of spiritual memory and continuation of consciousness that Goethe portrayed pictorially at the end of the eighteenth century, in the fairy tale about *The Green Snake and the Beautiful Lily*. For this purpose, the whole human being, in spirit, soul and body, must be actively engaged and transformed and its various forces must work together.

By the time the first edition of *The New Experience of the Supersensible* was published in 1995, the construction of the bridge could be described only up to a certain stage. We could report about the construction of the first half of the bridge stretching from head to heart, and from the etheric to the astral worlds. Only a few indications could be given concerning the more advanced stages of the bridge, leading from the heart to the metabolic-limb system and from the soul to the spiritual worlds and back to the body. These stages are described in the new edition of *The New Experience of the Supersensible.*

As we showed above, the seed of the entire bridge was laid in the encounter with *The Philosophy of Freedom*. We discovered that the free activity of thinking brings us to the middle point between the given and voluntary meetings with the Christ, the abyss of the Threshold between the physical and supersensible states of consciousness. We emphasized that imaginative perception is given as part of the first meeting with the Christ, but the spiritualization of pure thinking through *The Philosophy of Freedom* depends entirely on our free spiritual activity. Furthermore, it was discovered that the spiritualization of thinking also transforms the given imaginative *perception* into voluntary imaginative *cognition* by impregnating it with its clarity and precision. The spiritualization of thinking and the transformation of the given imaginative perception can be actualized only in the physical world, in the age of the Consciousness Soul.

When the Consciousness Soul is spiritualized by means of *The Philosophy of Freedom* and the Michaelic Yoga, this newest soul member becomes the Imaginative Soul, as Rudolf Steiner called it. In the Imaginative Soul, spiritualized thinking and the given imaginative perception merge and exchange their essences, to form modern imaginative cognition. This thought-permeated, imaginative cognition carries the clarity and freedom gained in the physical world to the spiritual world, and therefore can also carry the supersensible knowledge gained in the spiritual world, back to the physical world. In this way, spiritualized thinking, extracted from *The Philosophy of Freedom*, becomes the foundation of the self-conscious bridge between the physical and the higher worlds in the present Age of Michael. Therefore, it will be helpful, for the understanding of the spiritual science, art and craft of the bridge construction, used in the knowledge drama, to be reminded of how Rudolf Steiner characterized the spiritual significance of spiritualized thinking in the anthroposophical spiritual path.

In his main book, *Occult Science*, Rudolf Steiner writes that 'those who can allow it [pure thinking] to act upon them, will be following a safe and wholesome path and can thus win for themselves a feeling concerning the higher worlds, which will for all future time ensure for them most abundant results'. And further:

> By really thinking, one finds oneself already in the region of a living supersensible world. One says to oneself, 'there is something in me that fashions a thought organism; I am, nevertheless, at one with this something'. By surrendering oneself to sense-free thinking one becomes conscious of the existence of something essential flowing into our inner life... 'Something real proclaims its presence in me that binds thought to thought, fashioning a thought organism'. ...The observer who has surrendered himself to sense-free thought feels the spiritual reality announcing itself as though it existed within him, he feels himself one with it... one may then say, 'I remain quite silent within myself; I produce no thought associations; I surrender myself to what "thinks in me."' Then one is fully justified in saying, 'Something possessing the nature of being acts within me'... the thoughts are, indeed, already present when one surrenders to them; but one cannot think them if one does not, in every case, re-create them anew within the soul.[93]

---

[93] *Occult Science*, Chapter 5, 'Concerning Initiation' (GA 13). This experience is the foundation on which the knowledge drama of the Second Coming is based, and the spiritual steel of the infrastructure that holds the entire bridge construction together.

When pure thinking is developed to the level in which the cosmic thinking 'thinks in me', we gain a twofold experience and understanding concerning the significance of thinking. On the one hand, we understand how spiritualized thinking relates to imaginative perception, described above, and on the other, how it relates to ordinary thinking. It is placed in the middle between the two, and sheds new light on both, by bridging the abyss between them. As we saw, on the higher spiritual side of the abyss, spiritualized thinking unites with imaginative perception and transforms it by its unique qualities into the new, clear, and precise, controlled and regulated, imaginative cognition. This imaginative cognition is applied to the spiritual-scientific investigation of the meeting with the etheric Christ.

On the other hand, towards the physical side, spiritualized thinking transforms ordinary thinking and self-consciousness. The ordinary perception of the 'I' is given to us in physical life thanks to the incarnation in a physical body. Therefore, with the spiritualization of ordinary thinking, self-consciousness is also spiritualized and, furthermore, it becomes one with the stream of cosmic thinking and imaginative cognition. In this stream, that flows from below upwards, ordinary self-consciousness is spiritualized into *spiritual* self-consciousness, in which the 'I' knows itself as a spiritual 'I'. As spiritualized thinking transforms the given imaginative perception it also spiritualizes ordinary thinking and self-consciousness. This spiritual nature of thinking, that transforms both the physical and supersensible states of consciousness, is therefore the first stage in the construction of the human-cosmic bridge. It becomes its future seed, and all the higher spiritual forces developed in the knowledge drama of the Second Coming are rooted, nourished, and fostered continuously by the life stream of human-cosmic thinking.

The pivotal point, from which the bridge construction starts, and on which it is founded, is described by Rudolf Steiner in an addition to the ninth chapter, in the second edition of *The Philosophy of Freedom*:

> An important question, however, emerges here. If the human body has no part in the *essential nature* of thinking, what is the significance of this body within the whole nature of man? Now, what happens in this body through thinking has indeed nothing to do with the essence of thinking, but it has a great deal to do

with the arising of the self-consciousness out of this thinking. Thinking, in its own essential nature, certainly contains the real 'I' or Ego, but it does not contain the self-consciousness... The 'I' is to be found within the thinking; the 'self-consciousness' arises through the traces which the activity of thinking engraves upon our general consciousness, in the sense explained above. (The self-consciousness thus arises through the bodily organization. However, this must not be taken to imply that the self-consciousness, once it has arisen, remains dependent on the bodily organization. *Once arisen, it is taken up into thinking and shares henceforth in thinking's spiritual being.*)[94]

For the knowledge drama of the Second Coming, the pivotal point is clearly indicated here. First, it is pointed out that 'thinking, in its own essential nature, certainly contains the real "I" or Ego'. Second, 'once [self-consciousness] has arisen, it is taken up into thinking and shares henceforth in thinking's spiritual being'. The most important point is to realize the reciprocal flow and essence exchange between the essential spiritual nature of thinking, that contains the real 'I', and ordinary self-consciousness, reflected by the brain. Both the essential nature of thinking in which the real 'I' lives, and ordinary self-consciousness, reflected by the brain, are transformed at the same time by the activity of pure thinking. The real 'I' that lives in spiritualized thinking, and self-consciousness, that arises through the body, exchange their essential elements with each other. But what does this exchange truly mean?

It means that this transformation is reciprocal, and that each offers the other an essential element of itself, and each contains from now on the other's essence in its own essence. Above we called this process, 'essence exchange'.[95] Here it takes place between ordinary thinking and spiritualized thinking, between ordinary self-consciousness and the real 'I'. Ordinary self-consciousness, created by the physical body, is 'taken up' into the being of 'it thinks in me' of cosmic thinking, and 'shares henceforth in thinking's spiritual

---

[94] *The Philosophy of Freedom*, Chapter 9, 'The Reality of Freedom' (GA 4). First italics in original.

[95] See also *Die Philosophie der Freiheit als Grundlage künstlerischen Schaffens*, by Herbert Witzenmann, especially *Zweiter Teil*: 'Die Philosophie der Freiheit als Schulungsweg des Künstlers, 4. Der Wesenstausch, Selbstbewußtsein' (Gideon Spicker, 1988).

being', in which the real spiritual being of the 'I' is contained; and cosmic thinking, that 'in its own essential nature, certainly contains the real "I" or Ego, but not the self-consciousness', becomes self-conscious, and with it also the spiritual 'I' becomes self-conscious. This is the reason why this part of the bridge is so solid and robust, and why in this mutual essence exchange, the first foundation of the bridge of spiritual memory and continuation of consciousness is formed.

The activity of spiritualized thinking and the *self-conscious spiritual 'I'* that it forms, *cannot be forgotten*, whether we live in the physical or spiritual worlds. They accompany us in the physical and spiritual worlds, and in each moment, here and there, when we activate them, we become conscious of our whole human being, from both sides of the abyss of the Threshold. And this discovery becomes crucial in the transition from the given to the voluntary meeting with Christ, because the first stage of the knowledge drama means to individualize the gift of Christ's 'I' and let it dwell in full self-consciousness, in the free human 'I'. Let us describe this process further, to underline some of its essential elements.

Ordinary thinking is only a personal, subjective process, reflected by the physical brain, enclosed in the limits of the skull and ordinary self-consciousness. When we think in the physical world, we use the physical brain as an instrument and mirror, and therefore the form of ordinary thinking is determined by the physical brain. And the content and substance of thinking, which is taken originally out of the living cosmic thinking, is devitalized and killed in the brain. The earthly form of thinking, given by the brain, and the devitalized and despiritualized content of thinking are transformed into purely earthly formations.

When thinking is spiritualized, it takes leave of the physical brain and uses only the etheric brain, transforming form and content at the same time. The form and content of thinking are no longer reflected and devitalized in the physical brain. The content of thinking returns to its original spiritual state, resurrected as a living cosmic thought content, and is experienced in its primordial vibrant and radiant being. And when spiritualized thinking unites with the cosmic stream of thinking, it gives it a new form: a human-cosmic form.

This form is a new creation in the universe, that would not have come into being if man didn't create it on earth with the force of cosmic thinking. From a certain moment—that must be exactly grasped and delimited in full consciousness—the spiritual content and formative activity of cosmic thought spiritualizes the physical form of thinking and resurrects its killed content. From this moment, the form of thinking is no longer determined by the physical brain, but by the etheric brain, and taken up by the astral body and Ego. And the content of thinking is no longer the mere dead logical skeleton of earthly thinking, but the vibrant light-filled life of cosmic thinking.

From this stage, the form and content of thinking alike are transformed and transubstantiated in the etheric body and stream out into the higher worlds. The form of spiritual activity and the content of spiritual perception consist now of the same living substance and force. Both mutually determine and transform each other in this reciprocal essence exchange. Furthermore, the form of self-consciousness of the earthly 'I' is also transformed with the spiritualization of the form and content of thinking. In the free human-cosmic formation of cosmic thought, the active 'I' becomes conscious of its real spiritual being and substance. Therefore, when cosmic thinking 'thinks *in* me' it also 'thinks *me*', forms and transforms me into its cosmic likeness. Now it is not 'I' that thinks, because it is not the ordinary 'I' that forms this content; the content flows into my real spiritual 'I' from the cosmos when I spiritualize my thinking and lift it to the etheric brain; the free activity of the thinking 'I' is permeated and spiritualized by the spiritual flow of cosmic thought. But this also transforms the content and form of cosmic thought itself. While the 'I' is spiritualized by cosmic thinking, cosmic thinking is reciprocally individualized through the free activity of the thinking 'I'.

This reciprocal transformation of human and cosmic thinking is the fundamental activity of acquiring spiritual knowledge, that makes modern spiritual science into modern science. It is the gift of Michael to humanity in his present age, and thanks to this gift, the given meeting with the Christ can be transformed into the fully conscious meeting, in which the mystery of the 'I' gift is known and individualized. In the language of *The Philosophy of Freedom*, this process can be also described as follows.

'Intuitive thinking,' writes Rudolf Steiner, is a 'spiritual percept grasped without a physical organ.' This is experienced immediately, when we use only our etheric brain to think. Now, says

Rudolf Steiner further, this fully spiritualized thinking, 'is a percept in which the perceiver is himself active' and 'a self-activity which is at the same time perceived'.[96] These mysterious words that Rudolf Steiner added in 1918 to the second edition of *The Philosophy of Freedom*, contain a secret of true spiritual cognition and knowledge, that cannot be experienced by ordinary thinking. The first stage of the knowledge drama is founded on this fact, because this self-determining, self-reliance on spiritual activity, is the only guarantee of true freedom in the spiritual world. It makes spiritualized thinking into the bridging force between human thinking and imaginative cognition. In this way, *The Philosophy of Freedom* becomes the midwife and formative force of the new spiritual cognition.

But what does Rudolf Steiner really mean by the above-cited riddle? He refers to the simultaneous and reciprocal *spiritualization* of human thinking, and *individuation* of cosmic thinking. When he says that intuitive thinking 'is a percept' he means that the real 'I' perceives cosmic thought as the content of thinking. And in the experience of the cosmic thought content, 'the perceiver is himself active', because the real 'I' brings forth this thought content through the activity of intuitive thinking. Therefore, when 'a self-activity... is at the same time perceived', cosmic thought perceives itself—through the real 'I'—and is individualized. In any real spiritual activity, bringing forth spiritual content and perceiving it, is enacted, perceived, and known, as a mutually determined and reciprocated process.

In the etheric body, the active spiritualization of thinking and the passive reception and perception of cosmic thinking, become one reciprocal process of essence exchange: spiritualized thinking is penetrated by cosmic thinking, it becomes human-cosmic thinking, and cosmic thinking becomes cosmic-human thinking. Outside human activity, cosmic thinking is not self-conscious, it is integrated with all other cosmic beings and events; it gains self-consciousness through the real 'I', at the same time in which the human 'I' becomes conscious that he is a spiritual being. The human 'I' perceives cosmic thinking, it individualizes it; it gains from cosmic thinking the knowledge of its spiritual essence, and becomes this essence, and gives its self-consciousness to cosmic thinking. The 'I' is permeated by the cosmic substance of thinking,

---

[96] *The Philosophy of Freedom*, 'The Consequences of Monism' (GA 4).

through which it actualizes its spiritual being, and gives cosmic thinking its individualized human form. The 'I' is made cosmic, and cosmic thinking is individualized.

In this way, through the spiritualization of thinking, the Ur-phenomena of the mystery of *essence exchange*, taking place between the human 'I' and cosmic thinking, is actualized for the first time. It transforms both, and creates a wholly new human-cosmic, cosmic-human, being in the universe. In this manner, *The Philosophy of Freedom* creates the formative force and etheric organs of knowledge required for the reception and individuation of the Christ-'I' by the free human 'I', that constitutes the first stage of the knowledge drama of the Second Coming.[97] It forms the template on which the given meeting is transformed into a voluntary meeting and the first unconscious entry into the Grail Castle is transformed into the fully conscious second entry.

In the meeting with the etheric Christ in the modern Christ experience, the spiritual percept is not cosmic thought content but the given 'I' of Christ. In the first meeting, this 'I' can only be perceived and experienced. In the second meeting, the etheric heart organ, created in the spiritualization of thinking by the real 'I', becomes the conscious receiver of this 'I'. The real 'I' perceives the given 'I' as it is given and perceives itself as its self-conscious receiver. It is self-conscious in this intercourse activity, in the act of giving and receiving, and in the reciprocal relations between the giver—the Christ—and the human receiver; it is active as an independent spiritual being in its giving and reception.

Through spiritual activity and organs formed through the spiritualization of thinking and self-consciousness, described above, the giving and receiving of the 'I' of Christ becomes a fully conscious process. The task of the knowledge drama is therefore to receive and conceive, individualize, and recapitulate this giving and receiving process as a whole and transform the given 'I' into an indwelling 'I' in the human 'I'.

---

[97] In this manner, *The Philosophy of Freedom* fulfils the mission of thinking in the evolution of human consciousness, which is to endow the free thinking 'I' with immortal spiritual form and substance, that becomes the foundation of the continuation of spiritual memory and consciousness, that bridges day and night, life and death, and eventually also extends from one incarnation to the next.

The above-described essence exchange between ordinary and cosmic thinking, ordinary and spiritual self-consciousness, is the free human creation of the form and content that actualize the transformation process of the first into the second meetings with the Christ. This process is the conscious individuation of the given 'I' and its transformation into the indwelling 'I'. Then the 'I' of Christ can dwell in the etheric heart, together with the free human 'I', and the freedom of the human 'I' is not limited by its presence. Because this freedom is gained through the spiritualization of *The Philosophy of Freedom*, and the spiritualized being of *The Philosophy of Freedom* is the heart organ in which it dwells, human freedom is infinitely enhanced by the indwelling 'I'. In the thought-permeated imaginative cognition, one perceives the objective fact that the 'I' of Christ is active in the human 'I', as Paul experienced it: 'not my "I" is active and perceiving, but the "I" of Christ is active and perceives in my "I"'. This personal-impersonal perception guarantees human freedom and because it is actualized in the etheric heart, it also becomes the fountain of true love.

During the development of the knowledge drama, over more than three decades, we formed and applied specific meditative exercises, to intensify the reception and conception of the given 'I', to give it the most lucid and conscious imaginative formation. This process requires the constant supply of energizing and vivifying heart forces, of living spiritual nourishment, to enable its continuous development. An indicative example of such practice is presented below as Prelude to the detailed descriptions of the formation of the true 'I', in the fifth chapter of the new edition of *The New Experience of the Supersensible*. This practice actualizes the 'I' power that constitutes the foundation stone on which the entire bridge construction rests. We use it whenever we need to deepen the *will and heart* forces in which the self-conscious spiritual 'I' is grounded, and this must be done in each stage and step anew. To accomplish this, we kindle the fire of the will and heart forces that drive pure thinking, first actualized by *Johann Gottlieb Fichte*, the founding rock of the German Folk Spirit in its short incarnation in the eighteenth–nineteenth centuries.

As we showed above, the Platonic-Aristotelian essence exchange brings together two aspects of Rudolf Steiner's spiritual-scientific work that, though separated from each other in time, spring from the same deeper life source of anthroposophy as a whole. These two are his *first* philosophical and scientific works (1886-93) and the *last* ones (1917-24). The middle year through which the two periods are mutually crossed is 1908 (1892-1908-1924), in which the article *Philosophy and Anthroposophy* was written, where the sentence is found: 'Fichte may at this point supplement Aristotle.'[98] The true middle of spiritual science is actualized, therefore, by uniting the beginning of Rudolf Steiner's work, represented by *The Philosophy of Freedom*, and the Aristotelian last period, inaugurated with *The Riddles of the Soul* of 1917, through Fichte's impulse.

Rudolf Steiner dedicated his doctoral thesis, *Truth and Knowledge*, to placing Fichte's theory of knowledge on sound philosophical foundations. Fichte's great accomplishment was his discovery of the activity and actualization of the human 'I' in what he called the *Tathandlung* or *activity-act* of pure thinking. In this way, Fichte individualized, for the first time in human evolution, the active divine idea, or entelechy, that Aristotle applied only to God, to the free actively of the thinking 'I'. 'To Aristotle the idea of God is a pure actuality, a pure act, that is, an act in which actuality (the formative element) possesses the power to produce its own reality; it does not stand apart from matter, but by reason of its own activity fully and immediately coincides with reality'.

Through Fichte's continuously creative activity or *Tathandlung*, 'when we grasp the "I" in pure thought, we are in a centre where pure thought produces its own essential "matter" ...The "I" lives within itself; it produces its own concept and lives therein as a reality. *The activity of pure thought is not immaterial to the "I", for pure thought is the creator of the "I"'.*[99] These are epoch-making words if we experience that they express real spiritual *deeds*. For this reason, Rudolf Steiner could also say that 'the way in which Fichte characterizes the "I am" is wholly in the sense of occult science. Even though he remains in the field of pure thinking, his experience is not a mere speculation, but true inner experience. *Fichte leads thinking to the summit, from which one can enter the land of occult science.* And the preparation that one can achieve through him, is the purest of all.'[100]

---

[98] *Philosophy and Anthroposophy* (GA 35).

[99] Ibid. My italics.

[100] *Philosophy and Anthroposophy, Theosophy in Germany in the Previous Century* (GA 35). My italics.

Powerful will and heart forces are developed in this activity of the 'I' in pure thinking and are immensely fruitful for the bridge-building work. During this work, we felt repeatedly the drive, in specific moments, to 'Fichtezieren', as Novalis used to say, whenever he wanted to refresh his spiritual forces and delve again into the pure fountain of Fichte's thinking. For this purpose, we intensify and develop the dialectical gymnastics of Fichte between the 'I' and the 'Not-I', not in order to gain more knowledge about its meaning, which belongs elsewhere, but as spiritual exercises, aimed at actualizing the spiritual fullness of the 'I' in the activity of pure thinking. Then we extract from this activity the forces required to gain a secure and clear, indeed, the purest cognitive foundation to individualize the reception and conception of Christ's 'I' in the human 'I'.

We were striving to actualize in this way the *Tathandlung* to enhance the *Freiheitsakt* of *The Philosophy of Freedom*, as the fundamental activity-act of freedom in the present Age of Michael and place it in the service of the modern Christ experience. The result of this activity is that the spiritualized 'I', actualized in the pure act of thinking, can fully unite itself with Christ's given 'I' and transform it into the self-conscious indwelling 'I'. And this indwelling 'I' is the actual builder of the bridge of spiritual memory and continuation of consciousness in the knowledge drama of the Second Coming.

In other words, when the spiritualized thinking of *The Philosophy of Freedom*, enhanced through Fichte, transforms the given imaginative perception, it also transforms how we receive and individualize the gift of the 'I', that Christ offers to humanity today. For the first time in human evolution, in the age of the Consciousness Soul, through Michael's impulse, the given 'I' of Christ can be individualized through spiritualized thinking. The self-conscious spiritual 'I', formed through spiritualized thinking, becomes the self-conscious receiver of Christ's 'I'. When this happens, a new 'I' is formed, the child of Christ's 'I' and the self-conscious spiritual human 'I'. The new 'I' born of the union of the 'I' of Christ and the human 'I', their common child, is the *indwelling* 'I' of Christ, that lives and weaves self-consciously in the spiritual 'I'. And this indwelling 'I' becomes the first form in which the 'I' of Christ is individualized in the human 'I', and as Rudolf Steiner said, when the Christ 'enters into our own self... then with him in us we shall always be conscious of "Christ in us".' He becomes in the human 'I' 'the light that streams out in us... because in us, in our own being He becomes this light' and 'this gives the insight of the Christ-Being in our own self'.

With these words Rudolf Steiner indicates a momentous event, that begins in the knowledge drama of the Second Coming. 'It becomes an *indwelling insight,* an insight that dwells within the human being.'[101] The indwelling 'I' is the first born, true 'I' of man, the result of the free individuation of Christ's 'I' seed, given as a gift of grace in the first meeting. After we individualize this given 'I' in the knowledge drama of the Second Coming, it leads us to the second meeting, because only through the forces of the indwelling 'I' in us—not through our own 'I'—can we meet the Christ again.

The potential of the indwelling insight of the indwelling 'I' is the first golden seed given by the Christ. When we consciously actualized this power in our 'I', the two other golden seeds can be also activated and individualized in the knowledge drama. In the first stage, the indwelling insight active in our 'I' endows the human 'I' and soul with the new supersensible faculties of knowledge. Because our current conceptions of 'knowledge' are purely intellectual, it must be emphasized that the source of the new spiritual faculties of knowledge are the new forces of spiritualized love. Christ's indwelling insight, the source of the new forces of spiritual cognition, given by His indwelling 'I', is the light of love, and this love is a creative power. And this creative power of love can penetrate deep into the soul and bodily forces and spiritualize them.

We can only point in this Prelude to one aspect of this spiritualization process of the soul and bodily forces, the details of which are described in the new edition of *The New Experience of the Supersensible.* The power by means of which we transform spiritual knowledge based on love, into the creative power of love, that spiritualizes the soul and bodily forces, is found in what is called in

---

[101] Lecture of 14 September 1924 (GA 346). My italics. The light of the indwelling 'I', the 'indwelling insight' is the source of all supersensible seeing, perceiving, knowing, and doing in the higher worlds and on earth, which is the Christ-given light of the holy spirit, the spirit of modern spiritual science. The second and third stages of the giving and indwelling of the 'I', described by Rudolf Steiner in this lecture, are described in the second and third stages of the given Christ experience in Chapter 4, and their individuation is described in the construction of the second and third layers of the bridge, described in Chapter 5.

spiritual science 'the etherization of the blood'. In the knowledge
drama, this process is actualized in the free etheric heart, after the
etheric breathing of the Michaelic Yoga is established in the rhythmic system, and after the etheric head, heart and limbs become
organs of imaginative cognition.[102]

The above-described spiritualization of thinking, by means of
which the individuation of Christ's 'I' is taking place in the real
'I', also fires and intensifies the natural etherization process of the
blood. The indwelling 'I' dwells in the etheric heart, and from there
it irradiates and transforms the entire human constitution, in spirit,
soul and body. In this way, when the 'I' of Christ knows himself in
us, Christ's etherized blood also breathes and pulses in our 'I', soul,
and bodies. The indwelling 'I' becomes not only an indwelling
force of spiritual light and knowledge, but also a creative power,
that spiritualizes the various aspects of the soul and bodies.

In the course of the knowledge drama, the power of the indwelling 'I', used by the self-conscious real 'I', gradually penetrates and
transforms the forces of the soul and bodies. It gains the power to
spiritualize not only the soul forces of thinking, feeling and will,
but also the astral, etheric, and physical bodies. Through this activity the indwelling 'I' forms for itself new spiritual, soul, and physical forces, members, and bodies.

To begin with, the pure soul activity, 'the creator of the "I"', irradiates, penetrates and spiritualizes the astral body, in which the
'I' dwells, and brings about the transformation of the astral body
to *Spirit Self*. Spirit Self is the astral body that the 'I' has spiritualized by means of its free cognitive and moral activity, as we shall
show below in greater detail when we describe the meeting with
Anthroposophia. Further, the 'I' can intensify and deepen its spiritual activity, supported now by the spiritualized part of the astral
body, to penetrate the etheric body, and the part of the etheric body
that is spiritualized in this way, becomes the seed of the *Life Spirit*,
that consists of pure, eternal spiritual life.

And the 'I' can also intensify its spiritual activity to such an
extent, that its spiritual force also spiritualizes the physical body.
This happens to the extent that the activity of the 'I', powered
by the indwelling 'I' of Christ, works directly into the forces of

---

[102] The transformation of the etheric body is described in *Cognitive Yoga* and
in the new edition of *The New Experience of the Supersensible*.

breathing and blood circulation. This happens through the *warmth of devotion* that fires the will and heart forces that motivate pure thinking. Then it 'affects the circulation of the blood', because of the 'Christ influence expressing itself in a special form of circulation, penetrating even the physical principle'. In place of the old initiations that required the unconscious separation of the etheric body from the physical body by the hierophant, during the three-and-a-half day death-like sleep, today man can 'be initiated within the physical body: the Christ-Impulse has the power to bring this about'; and if we embody this impulse consciously through the spiritual activity of the 'I', we 'see it so spiritually alive that it acts as a force communicating itself even to his circulation'. In this way, 'such a man achieves through this experience the same result that was formerly brought about by the withdrawal of the etheric body'.[103]

This effect becomes strongly potentized if the 'I' of Christ is individualized in the spiritualized thinking of *The Philosophy of Freedom*, intensified through the will and heart forces of Fichte. Then we experience how 'through the Christ impulse something has come to earth which enables the human being to influence the force that causes his blood to pulsate through his body. What is here active is... solely *the mighty influence of the Christ-Individuality*', planted as an 'I' seed in the human 'I' in the etheric meeting with the Christ. 'Through the spirit that streams forth as the Christ impulse, something flows into the body, something that can otherwise be induced only by way of psycho-physiological development through fire: an inner fire expressing itself in the circulation of the blood... if a man opens his soul to the Christ impulse, this impulse acts in such a way that *the experiences of the astral body flow over into the etheric body, and clairvoyance results*'.[104]

In other words, this means that the conscious individuation of the 'I' of Christ is not a mystical event experienced only in the soul, but a *chemical* event. Therefore, it is not a 'mystical wedding' but a 'chemical wedding', inaugurated in Christian Rosencreuz's initiation, because the free spiritual activity of the 'I', working through thinking, feeling and will, spiritualizes and transubstantiates, not

---

[103] Lecture of 30 June 1909 (GA 112).

[104] Ibid. My italics. This process is described in detail in the new edition of *The New Experience of the Supersensible*.

only the soul forces and members but also the three bodies, including the physical body.

As Rudolf Steiner showed, such an intensified spiritual activity, fired by the heart and will forces of the 'I', brings to consciousness the otherwise unconscious process of the etherization of the blood, and in this way the etheric Christ is perceived in modern imaginative cognition. 'Spiritual science must... fire the streams [of Christ's etherized blood] flowing from heart to brain... If this comes to pass, individuals will be able to comprehend the event that has its beginning in the twentieth century: the appearance of the etheric Christ'.[105]

As demonstrated also in *Cognitive Yoga*, the same etherization process that creates the forces to perceive the etheric Christ, also opens the way to experience the whole etheric body, and in the new edition of *The New Experience of the Supersensible*, we describe how the etherized blood is used to also spiritualize the *physical* body. 'That which shall be given as the new Mystery schooling will reveal the Mystery of the living Christ in a new *way, through the transformation of the physical body*'.[106]

This must be emphasized especially in our time, in which 'spiritual' is often misconstrued as a merely psychological force and the spirituality of the body is ignored. But for true spiritual science, the very opposite holds true. The physical body, which is considered 'the lowest' body in our constitution, is the most evolved and perfect, and was created by the highest spiritual beings. And the Christ penetrated, spiritualized, and resurrected the astral, etheric and physical bodies of Jesus, and spiritualized them into Spirit Self, Life Spirit and Spirit Man, completing the divine archetype of humanity, that is developing gradually from old Saturn to Vulcan. This power makes it possible to experience in our own body the first dawn of Christ's resurrection body, the 'Phantom'. But the magical power that awakens the golden seed of the Phantom, given by the Christ, must be, in the present age, the activity of spiritualized thinking, through which the 'I' penetrates to the spiritual foundations of the astral, etheric, and physical bodies. This is one of the deepest secrets of esoteric Christianity, of the Grail and the Rosicrucian streams, and Rudolf Steiner hoped that future anthroposophy

---

[105] Lecture of 1 October 1911 (GA 130).
[106] Lecture of 17 June 1910 (GA 121). My italics.

will realize it in the epoch of the Consciousness Soul, through the spiritual activity stimulated by Michael, fired by the forces of the etheric Christ in the Second Coming.

As we show in the new edition of *The New Experience of the Supersensible*, in the knowledge drama this activity becomes so intense, that when the 'I' spiritualizes the etheric warmth forces in the heart, it also spiritualizes the *physical* warmth, and as it gains increased strength, it can also spiritualize the forces of light ether in the air element, through which the spiritualized part of the astral body, the Spirit Self, works. And if the 'I' intensifies its activity further, it can spiritualize the etheric body that works through the chemical ether and the fluid element and use the forces of Life Spirit to also spiritualize the life ether that informs the physical body, in which Spirit Man is working. Then the four members and bodies, etheric forces and elements become pregnant and productive, fructified by the indwelling power of Christ's 'I' in the human 'I'.

In the past only initiated persons, like Jacob Boehme, could still experience a reminiscence of this mystery. 'The earthly body is the *mysterium*, wherein the arcanum lies in great hiddenness... our old Adam and body is the origin of the new body, because it is the mother: out of the old substance arises the new body'.[107] And the resurrected body, also called *Phantom* in spiritual science, is the body formed by and for the indwelling 'I', as the physical body is formed to reflect ordinary self-consciousness. It becomes the perfect spiritual mirror, that reflects the spiritual 'I' that creates it and lifts it to the light of full spiritual self-conscious.[108]

In this way, the spiritual 'I' builds for itself, in self-conscious spiritual activity, three spiritualized bodies, that constitute the threefold bridge, through which it recapitulates the given Christ experience in a conscious way. And when during the knowledge

---

[107] Jacob Böhme, *Vierzig Fragen von der Seele*, Amsterdam 1648, 16: 6, p. 109; *Von Menschwerdung Jesu Christi*, Amsterdam 1682, 2, 10:2, p. 163.

[108] 'The whole evolution of humanity was threatened with the danger that the Ego-consciousness would be lost... Everything that depends on perfect reflection from the physical body would have become increasingly worn out... [the Phantom] signifies literally the rescue of the human Ego'. (Lecture of 11 October 1911, GA 131.) The third, spiritual-physical layer of the bridge, is constituted by the Phantom, as we show in *The New Experience of the Supersensible*.

drama, the given meeting and 'I' giving by the Christ is recapitulated consciously, Christ's indwelling 'I' becomes the Gate[109] that
leads to the meetings with Michael and Anthroposophia.

This is the goal of the knowledge drama of the Second Coming,
to 'alchemically' transform the three soul forces and members and
the three bodies, to form the chalice that receives the Ego of the
Christ, contain, and nourish it, and reflect it in the light of clear
spiritual knowledge. This enables us 'to get to know the mystery
of the Christ-Ego, the eternal ego into which any human ego can
be transformed... as a given fact so that man can receive the Christ-
Ego at the sight of the Holy Grail'.[110]

---

[109] 'I AM the gate; whoever enters through me will be saved; They will
come in and go out and find pasture', John 10:9.
[110] Lecture of 11 April 1909 (GA 109).

Chapter 7
The Meeting with Michael

A deeply moving spiritual experience takes place after the knowledge drama of the Second Coming has reached a certain stage, and the given meeting with the etheric Christ is individualized and recapitulated consciously. We feel that we draw ever closer to the spiritual being of Michael, the source of spiritual science. Only very gradually could we begin to experience the real spiritual beings that stand behind the inherited form of spiritual science, created a century ago by Rudolf Steiner.

Previously, all our forces had been concentrated on the transformation of this earthly form, that covered its spiritual origins. This earthly form became increasingly hardened and impenetrable through a hundred years of physical life, and many obstacles had to be first surmounted, before we could experience the concrete spiritual beings behind it. The first direct contact with Michael took place, therefore, after decades of spiritual research. It happened when the practice of Michaelic Yoga freed the etheric body from the physical body, paved the way from the head to the heart, and formed the etheric heart organ described above. This organ, through which the second meeting with the Christ is actualized in the knowledge drama, was formed by Michael's 'new will of yoga' and therefore could also eventually perceive it in the external spiritual world. When this occurred, it opened the portal that leads to the cosmic will forces of Michael, and we could grasp them directly at their source.[111]

At this stage, the given 'I' of Christ is transformed into the indwelling 'I' and begins to act in our free 'I' as an independent spiritual being. It must be emphasized, to prevent misunderstandings, that this 'I' alone, not our ordinary 'I' and not our spiritual 'I', brings

---

[111] The experience of the spiritual beings behind the earthly form of spiritual science, took place at the transition from the last and the present century and was developed gradually in the first decade. My book *Cognitive Yoga* was already an expression of this development. This is also the reason for the late publication of the 2nd edition of *The New Experience of the Supersensible*, because some 30 years were required to raise the meeting with Michael and Anthroposophia to full consciousness.

about the meeting with Michael.[112] To begin with, the Michaelic Yoga is naturally actualized by our ordinary 'I', then it is taken hold of by our real spiritual 'I', forming the essence exchange of pure thinking and imagination, and then it becomes the life-giving breathing of the indwelling 'I'. It weaves together the streams of etheric exhalation and inhalation, and at the above-indicated stage on the path, we become aware that this spiritualized breathing merges with Michael's etheric breathing and heartbeat in the etheric world.

This takes place because this etheric breathing is the spiritual breathing of the indwelling 'I' in the etheric heart. At a certain singular moment, when the individuation of the 'I' of Christ is accomplished thus far, we experience *how* this breathing is happening, and above all, *whose* breathing it is. At this stage, the indwelling 'I' becomes the organ used by Michael to reveal himself directly to us. For example, we discover that when we breathe spiritually, cognitively, rhythmically, in this manner, through the essence exchange between spiritualized thinking and imaginative perception, we factually *breathe with Michael.* What is more, we discover that it is Michael himself who breathes in and through us, and that the entire human experience of this etheric breathing is an expression of a single, individualized, pulse and beat of his infinite cosmic breathing and heartbeat.

Indeed, one begins to experience Michael as the spirit that carries Christ's etheric breathing through the cosmos, as an expression of his own spiritual breathing; one feels that Michael's life- and light-radiating sun body, the source of his spiritual breathing, is the macrocosmic source and activity that breathes and pulses through our microcosmic etheric breathing in the Michaelic Yoga. The Michaelic Yoga, given by Rudolf Steiner in 1919-20, comes here to full expression. Rudolf Steiner's fiery Michaelic exclamation, 'We must develop this new yoga will!', now takes on a wholly new and concrete meaning.

---

[112] Such exact distinctions that may seem superfluous to the casual reader are absolutely required, if spiritual-scientific research is conducted in accord with the real science of the spirit as inaugurated by Rudolf Steiner. The clear distinction between the ordinary 'I', the spiritual 'I' and the indwelling 'I' of Christ, belongs to the most essential foundations of the knowledge drama, and constitute the basic structure and function of the 'threefold true "I"', whose formation and activity is described in detail in the new edition of *The New Experience of the Supersensible.*

We realize, furthermore, that the substance and rhythm of Michael's etheric breathing activity originate in a continuous etheric essence exchange with the cosmic life of the etheric Christ; what was described above as the etheric breathing between the imaginative perception of the etheric Christ and our spiritualized thinking, appears here in its macrocosmic light and significance. It appears as Michael's cosmic etheric breathing and pulsating heartbeat, that demonstrates, as a messenger of Christ, how he pours down his majestic cosmic Imaginations to humanity on the earth. We discover that it is Michael's cosmic yoga will that pulses through his breathing that flows through us, and lets us actualize in our etheric body the essence exchange between the human etheric body and the etheric body of the Christ, and between Christ's 'I' and the human 'I'. Then we realize that without being aware of this fact, from the first moment in which we began to spiritualize the intuitive thinking of *The Philosophy of Freedom* as a foundation of the Michaelic Yoga and knowledge drama, Michael was actively involved in each and every turn and phase of this process; but we couldn't yet sense and see his cosmic presence and activity, working through our activity, enlivening and animating it through and through.

Now we realize that the human actualization of the Michaelic Yoga is the microcosmic actualization of his cosmic yoga breathing, that our spiritual breathing is a drop or seed containing his radiating, rhythmically pulsating, life-giving sunlight. This becomes a real experience. It becomes the heartfelt source of cosmic-human intimacy, where a sacred meeting place between a god and the indwelling 'I' of Christ is consecrated.

From the beginning of the knowledge drama of the Second Coming, we used Michael's forces and did not perceive their real cosmic source. But the more the reception and individuation of Christ's 'I' progresses, the more this source lights up in imaginative consciousness, and we feel obliged to say to ourselves: Now we consciously partake in Michael's cosmic will of yoga, in his spiritual activity and consciousness, because he is the being that, in truth, incorporates and embodies himself in all our spiritualized thinking, perceiving, feeling and will, carefully stirring and shaping his spiritual breathing rhythms into our etheric breathing, and pulsing with his cosmic heartbeat through the human heartbeat, when we actualize his will of cosmic yoga.

Then we begin to understand from our own experience what Rudolf Steiner meant when he said the following:

> Human beings exist as mineral beings, live and thrive as plants, feel as animals, judge and draw conclusions as human beings, perceive as angels and, sixth, human beings behold the spiritual world that is, Imaginatively, as archangels. When we speak of the human being since the last third of the 19th century, we would have to acknowledge the following: we perceive as angels and develop the consciousness soul by means of soul faculties of vision—to begin with, unconsciously, but still as the consciousness soul—as archangels.[113]

This becomes a real experience in the knowledge drama, when the Consciousness Soul is transformed into the Imaginative Soul, and we, through Michael, 'imaginatively behold the spiritual world as Archangels'. But it takes time to realize, that the forces of *this* specific kind of imaginative vision, which is unique among all others, because it alone is fully penetrated and transformed by spiritualized thinking, are given by Michael. We learn to differentiate between the thought permeated and spiritualized imaginative cognition of Michael and the other kinds of imaginative perceptions.[114]

We experience the intimate connection that human beings can form in our time with Michael if they spiritualize their soul forces, through the spiritualization of thinking. 'Michael is the active Being, the Being who, as it were, pulses through our breath, our veins, our nerves, to the end that we may actively develop all that belongs to our full humanity in connection with the Cosmos.' This 'pulsing through our breath, veins and nerves' is no metaphor but spiritual

---

[113] Lecture of 2 June 1921 (GA 204). The Archangels develop the Life Spirit as their central spiritual member, and Michael's cosmic breathing is the expression of his cosmic Life Spirit. In the Michaelic Yoga, we perceive how Michael thinks and perceives, breathes, and pulses in the forces of our imagination, as their formative spiritual source.

[114] As a rule, the forces of supersensible perception are given by the other Archangels, notably by Mercury-Raphael and Uriel, and to a lesser extent also Gabriel, but Michael is concerned with inspiring the above-described forces of imagination, fertilized, and spiritualized by spiritual thinking, the offspring of his cosmic intelligence, that he supervises, as the son and director of the cosmic forces of wisdom of his Mother Sophia.

reality in the etheric world and body. We participate in Michael's own pulsing and breathing when we experience it inside our spiritualized breathing, nerves, and veins. Now the true spiritual reality that animates and inspires the practice of Michaelic Yoga through *The Philosophy of Freedom*, comes to light. 'What stands before us as a challenge of Michael is that *we become active in our very thoughts, working out our view of the world through our own inner activity.*'

In this way we make it possible for Michael to fulfil his cosmic mission as intermediary between humanity, Christ, cosmic Sophia, and the Hierarchies, which he considers as his main task in his present age. We feel his stark, affirmative fulfilment pulsing through the etheric forces of our thinking and perceiving, breathing and blood circulation. In doing so, we consciously unite with the sense of fulfilment that he has in carrying out his mission, because 'if Michael is to bring back the right message to the world of the Gods, he must speak to this effect: *During my Age, human beings have raised to the Supersensible what they developed in the way of thinking purely in terms of Space; and we can therefore accept human beings again, for they have united their thought with ours.*'[115] This intimate meeting with Michael became possible at the end of the twentieth century and the beginning of the twenty-first century. 'Before that time man could only feel how thoughts formed themselves in his own being; from the time indicated he is able to raise himself above his own being; he can turn his mind to the Spiritual; *he there meets Michael*, who proves his ancient kinship with everything connected with thought.'[116]

Since then, 'the science which as anthroposophical Spiritual Science again spiritualizes spatial thinking, lifts it again into the supersensible; this Spiritual Science works from below upwards, *stretches out its hands as it were from below upwards to grasp the hands of Michael stretching down from above. It is then that the bridge can be created between man and the Gods'.[117] And we experience during the formation of this bridge, in the knowledge drama of the Second Coming, that this intimate meeting with Michael takes place; we feel, when 'not "I" but the indwelling "I" of Christ' breathes

---

[115] Lecture of 17 December 1922 (GA 219). My italics.
[116] *Leading Thoughts*, 'At the Dawn of the Michael Age' (GA 26). The time to which Rudolf Steiner refers is the end of the nineteenth century, but until the end of the twentieth century, he remained alone in this experience.
[117] Lecture of 17 December 1922 (GA 219). My italics.

in and through us, how we stretch our etheric hands from below upward, and how they are grasped most gently by the etheric hands of Michael, that he stretches towards us from above downwards. We let the indwelling 'I', working through our spiritual 'I', exhale our spiritualized thinking, feeling and will forces and inhale Michael's cosmic thinking, feeling and will impulses, until we feel how he breathes through our spiritualized human breath, and how we breathe through his cosmic breath, as he wills, feels, and thinks in our etheric heart. Then we consciously co-create with him 'the bridge... between man and the Gods'.

In the etheric heart we also experience the urgent yearning of Michael to find a new dwelling place in a new earthly-human sun, because he left his cosmic abode in the sun at the end of the nineteenth century, when he descended to the earth to fulfil his new age, following the example of the Christ. We realize that he can only find his new sun abode on the earth in human hearts aglow with Christ's fire and light, in which the Christ dwells. We experience this in his sense of fulfilment that fills the atmosphere that emanates from his being since the meeting began. We feel his cosmic-human satisfaction, because 'he is seeking a new metamorphosis of his cosmic task. Formerly he allowed the thoughts to stream from the spiritual outer world into the souls of human beings; since the last third of the nineteenth century *he wishes to live in the human souls in which the thoughts are formed.*' But in the twentieth century, since Rudolf Steiner's death, his hopes have been disappointed again and again and his sorrow and worries about the fate of humanity reached a tragic culmination at the end of the century.

For Michael, the long hoped-for dawn of the new light from the sun becoming earth, appeared first at the end of the century. Only since the end of the last century, could he find it in the human hearts, in which the sun being of the Christ is dwelling, and only since then could he experience the fulfilment of his yearning for the first time. Because he had to wait until the new revelation of the etheric Christ would be first grasped and individualized with the help of his spiritualized intelligence, created in human hearts. This only occurs when 'the human beings related to Michael... *know that they ought to let Michael dwell in their hearts'.* This is the crucial and most intimate moment in the meeting with Michael, that we feel how he descends and dwells in our souls and unites with the indwelling 'I' of Christ in the etheric heart. We 'now dedicate to him the spiritual life which is based upon thought; now, in the free and individual life of thought, we allow ourselves to be instructed by Michael as to which are the right paths of the soul'.[118]

This takes place after Michael 'liberates thought from the sphere of the head; he clears the way for it to the heart; he enkindles enthusiasm in the feelings, so that the human mind can be filled with devotion for all that can be experienced in the *light of thought'*. This light of thought is the light of 'the indwelling insight', created by the indwelling 'I' of Christ in the human heart. And we can truly feel that at this moment indeed, 'the Age of Michael has dawned. Hearts are beginning to have thoughts; spiritual fervour is now proceeding, not merely from mystical obscurity, but from souls clarified by thought. To understand this means to receive Michael into the heart. Thoughts which at the present time strive to grasp the Spiritual must originate in hearts which beat for Michael as the fiery Prince of Thought in the Universe.'[119]

Only then can we invite Michael to dwell in our hearts and meet him face to face, when we experience him as 'the fiery Prince of Thought in the Universe', because we return his cosmic intelligence to him in our etheric hearts, where it becomes vibrantly alive and resurrected in the light of the spiritualized thinking of *The Philosophy of Freedom*, as 'love in its spiritual form'. And then, as a cordial gesture, in exchange for our offering him back his stolen intelligence redeemed from Ahriman, he allows us to experience and share—through his being—the cosmic source of his cosmic intelligence. This is another important event, that belongs to the meeting with Michael in his present age. Through him—and only through him is this possible today—he lets us also meet and experience his cosmic Mother, 'that powerful Being... Soph-Ea, Sophia... the all-pervading, omnipresent wisdom, sending to mankind her son... later called Micha-el'.[120]

The revelation of the cosmic Mother Sophia through her son Michael, takes place in the sacred shrine and altar of the etheric heart, in which the individualized 'I' of Christ dwells, formed through the etheric breathing of Michaelic Yoga. When this mystery is

[118] *Leading Thoughts,* 'At the Dawn of the Michael Age' (GA 26). My italics.
[119] Ibid.
[120] Lecture of 11 August 1924 (GA 243).

experienced, we feel how the cosmic Mother and her son jubilate, because 'the hearts of human beings... become the helpers of Michael in the conquering of the Intelligence that has fallen to the Earth'; because we overcame Ahriman in our spiritualized thinking, actualized and individualized the human-cosmic, cosmic-human intelligence, and returned it to its mother-source, it is now embodied, active, breathing and pulsating, in the human heart.

Since the end of the twentieth century, and increasingly with each year and decade in the twenty-first century, 'this battle, more than any other, is laid in the *human heart'*. What Rudolf Steiner said about the end of the nineteenth century and hoped for in the twentieth century, must be rephrased, and updated a century later. 'There, within the hearts of human beings, this battle has been waged since the last third of the *twentieth* century. Decisive indeed is what human hearts *have done* with this Michael Impulse in the *etheric* world in the twentieth century', while on the earth the worst eventuality took place. 'After the end of the twentieth century, when the first century after the end of Kali Yuga has elapsed, *and humanity fell into the grave of all civilization'*—this fact has been well established in current spiritual investigations—'the souls that participated in this battle in the etheric world during the twentieth century, will work on the earth for the resurrection of humanity from this grave of all civilization'. Only then would Rudolf Steiner's hopes be fulfilled, in the totally changed conditions after the apocalyptic twilight of humanity, namely, that 'at the beginning of that Age [in the twenty-first century] when in the souls of human beings who in their hearts ally Intelligence with Spirituality, Michael's battle will be fought out to victory'.[121]

Now, in the etheric human heart, in the indwelling 'I' of Christ, Michael finds his dwelling place, and his cosmic Mother, Sophia, is present through his presence; and the indwelling being of Michael unites in our heart with the indwelling being of Christ. Heavenly-earthly fulfilment and joy are experienced when this meeting commences, to use rather trivial earthly words, because Michael and Christ were separated from each other after the Christ left the sun

---

[121] Lecture of 19 July 1924 (GA 240). The apocalypse of the twentieth and twenty-first centuries, is described from various points of view in the *Twilight and Resurrection of Humanity: The History of the Michaelic Movement since the Death of Rudolf Steiner* (Temple Lodge, 2020).

before the Mystery of Golgotha. Christ has lived on earth since Golgotha and Michael remained in the sun until the end of the nineteenth century, when he began his descent to earth to fulfil his role in his new age. When human beings meet the etheric Christ and receive the 'I' of Christ into their hearts through the light of the modern Grail, spiritual science, they invite Michael to dwell in the sun forces of their hearts as well, and the two cosmic sun beings meet again—on earth—for the first time since their separation.

The meeting takes place in the free etheric hearts of human beings that live consciously in the etheric earthy-human sun, whose formation was described for the first time in *The Spiritual Event of the 20th Century*.[122] The joy of the reunion of Michael and Christ reverberates through the entire etheric sphere of the earthly-human sun. It lights its aura with marvellous colours and causes it to resound with deeply moving tones and wonderful melodies. And in this celebration, the new cosmic cultus and spiritual communion of humanity, described in the new edition of *The New Experience of the Supersensible*, is actualized. To use once more wholly inadequate earthly words, we feel invited to participate in the sacred and festive marriage of Michael and Christ, Christ and Sophia, in the temple of the human and planetary heart, in which they exchange their essences and fructify each other.

In this marriage something happens in human evolution, that can only happen in the present Age of Michael. From their union in our hearts, a new spiritual being is born. In this singular event, the cosmic wisdom, Sophia, is individualized as well. Her primordial cosmic light, that illuminates the meetings with the etheric Christ, through spiritual science, the gift of Michael, her son, to humanity, that became *Philo-Sophia* from Plato and Aristotle until *The Philosophy of Freedom*, becomes fully human. From the union of Christ and Michael-Sophia in the human heart, the sister of the indwelling 'I' is born, and takes her place in the human heart, as an independent spiritual being, the second offspring of the knowledge drama of the Second Coming.

---

[122] *The Spiritual Event of the 20th Century. The occult significance of the 12 years 1933-1945 in the light of spiritual science. An Imagination* (Temple Lodge 1996).

In the short present Age of Michael, in the middle, second century in which we live, this must be accomplished by a growing number of people, united in the new Michaelic community, the brotherhood and sisterhood of the true School of Michael. If this will be accomplished in the first part of this century by at least a small number of people, the second incarnation of Anthroposophia will have been prepared and a second major Michaelic impulse may be given to humanity during the twenty-first century.

Chapter 8
The Meeting with Anthroposophia

2500 years after the birth of Philo-Sophia out of the cosmic wisdom of Sophia and Michael, in Plato and Aristotle, and a century after Rudolf Steiner created the seed of anthroposophy in *The Philosophy of Freedom*, spiritualized thinking, 'love in its spiritual form', could become the mother of the new imaginative cognition. In the knowledge drama of the Second Coming, anthroposophy could unite with the newly developing supersensible faculties given by the etheric Christ. As we saw above, the Michaelic Yoga, that starts with the spiritualization of thinking and sense-perception, becomes conscious etheric breathing with Christ, actualized through the will of yoga of Michael. During the knowledge drama of the Second Coming, the etheric breathing with the Christ expands to include the etheric breathing of Michael, and a three-way etheric breathing comes about between Christ, man, and Michael. Michael's activity in the etheric heart allows man to breathe in the gift of the 'I' of Christ, and breathe out our spiritual activity, that he gracefully takes into himself. In this way we gradually individualize the gift of Christ's 'I' and let it dwell in the human 'I'. The indwelling 'I' forms the foundation of the supersensible bridge of spiritual memory and continuation of consciousness. The more we actualize this mutual breathing, the more Michael himself becomes visible, as his previously hidden activity comes to light. Then, as he opens the way to the second meeting with the Christ, he also kindles the 'indwelling insight' in the etheric heart, the light of spiritual knowledge, and reveals the presence of his cosmic mother, the Sophia of Christ, through his indwelling spiritual being and activity.

As Michael becomes visible and joins the Christ in the human heart, something else happens, that remained in the background all along. It lights up in supersensible cognition, when the etheric breathing and weavings of Michael through the human soul are experienced consciously. Until this point, the spiritual light that illuminated the first and second meetings with Christ, remained unilluminated, and is the last to be revealed. Only through the meeting with Michael, when Michael joins the indwelling 'I' of Christ in the etheric heart, is this light transformed into self-conscious spirit light as well. In complete selflessness, it poured itself to illuminate and bring to imaginative cognition the entire development of the knowledge drama of the Second Coming, being the living fabric of this supersensible knowledge process. But when Michael unites in our heart with the etheric Christ, and the light of cosmic Sophia radiates through this union, this light of spiritual knowledge is also individualized; it is born and revealed as an independent spiritual being. She becomes the second child of the sacred marriage of Christ and Sophia through Michael and takes her place in the human heart beside her elder brother, the indwelling 'I' of Christ.

It is important to note, that her elder brother, the indwelling 'I' of Christ, stands already by her side when she is born. He is the firstborn of the spiritual marriage and essence exchange between Christ and Michael in the human heart. The flames of sacred fire that fill the etheric heart with the bliss of spiritual warmth, and the light that illuminates this sacred union, are kindled by the 'indwelling insight' radiating from the indwelling 'I'. Its pure human source is revealed through the light of spiritualized thinking, after it became 'love in its spiritual form'. This force of love takes a spiritual body of her own and appears as the second child born from the marriage of Christ and Michael-Sophia in the human heart. She becomes visible when the indwelling insight of the indwelling 'I', her brother, becomes mature enough, that its forces, that were previously invested in the formation of the new imaginative cognition, are freed to illuminate their spiritual source. This source is now born, that is, revealed as a real spiritual being. It was by means of the spiritual light given by this hidden being that we could actualize and perceive the meetings with the Christ and Michael and unite their indwelling beings in our hearts.

To begin with, human beings only knew her shadow, the form she assumes in the given, earthly anthroposophy. And now she is resurrected and born again, and we meet her true spiritual being. She remained invisible so long as her light was wholly dedicated to illuminate the meetings and essence exchanges of the Christ and Michael in the etheric heart; now she comes to her light and her light illuminates also herself, and the invisible embodiment of anthroposophical spiritual knowledge becomes visible. Now this light, conceived and enhanced through this essence exchange, lets the invisible being at its source shine forth and reveal herself. Born in the union of Christ and Michael in the human heart, individualized through the spirit fire of the indwelling 'I', her light shines back and illuminates its source in her living being. Through the intimate union of the Christ and Michael, when the Sophia of Christ is fully present, that gives birth to the indwelling 'I' of Christ in the human heart, the light of spiritual knowledge is condensed and assumes wonderfully radiating, light-filled, human-cosmic form, that completes the fourfold formation of the holy human-divine family in the human soul and heart.

When she is born in the human heart, we also realize that this being is the source of the forces of pure thinking experienced through the spiritualization of *The Philosophy of Freedom*, the mother-source of the new imaginative cognition and spiritual self-consciousness, formed in the knowledge drama of the Second Coming. Now we meet this mother-source face to face and know her as an independent spiritual being for the first time, standing next to Christ and Michael and her elder brother, the indwelling 'I' in the human heart. Her abundant grace offers the purest forces of spiritual cognition that humanity must develop in this age, to bring the Michael-Christ mystery to full consciousness.

We feel that it would have been wholly unworthy, even despicable, to be tempted to grasp and interpret these sacred meetings and birth processes, with the analytic ahrimanic intellect and visionary and speculative luciferic forces. To approach the etheric meetings with Christ and Michael and celebrate their union in the right way, we must actualize again and again the virgin purity of Goethe's experience of the sense world, to save our perceptions and creative imagination from the pitfalls of Lucifer, and we redeem modern intellectual thinking through the virgin purity of *The Philosophy of Freedom*, that alone can save the fallen cosmic intelligence from Ahriman and return it to Michael and Sophia.

The Michaelic Yoga, as Rudolf Steiner conceived it in 1919-20, is based on this overcoming of Ahriman and Lucifer in all the forces of the human soul. When we actualize pure thinking and sense-perception in the Michaelic Yoga, we feel justified to say to ourselves: The knowledge of the Christ, the Sophia of Christ, must originate only from the purest virgin forces of the human soul. The forces of the astral body used to acquire this kind of imaginative knowledge, must be the purest expression of the pristine etheric and astral forces of the human being, to which the luciferic and ahrimanic forces have no access. Only these pristine virgin human and cosmic forces, dormant and protected through the ages in the deepest recesses of the human soul and bodies, should give birth to *this* force of knowledge; and these forces alone are worthy to become the life-giving modern 'Sophia of Christ'.

We should be reminded that what has been achieved since the end of the last century by means of the spiritualization of *The Philosophy of Freedom* in the knowledge drama of the Second Coming, is possible because of the forces given by the new revelation of the etheric Christ. It alone resurrects, enlivens, and spiritualizes thinking to such an extent, that its living power, enhanced through the Michaelic Yoga, also spiritualizes the given forces of imaginative perception. In this imaginative form, it begins to circulate in our etherized breathing and blood, illuminating the etheric meetings with Christ and Michael. In this practice, says Rudolf Steiner, we can progress 'very far in the matter of catharsis', provided we 'inwardly experience all that is contained in my book, *The Philosophy of Freedom*'. This happens when we succeed, by means of our own forces, to 'actually reproduce the thoughts just as they are there presented', as 'a virtuoso, in playing a selection on the piano, holds to the composer of the piece, that is, he reproduces the whole thing within himself'. Then 'catharsis will be developed to a high degree'. If we then combine the work with *The Philosophy of Freedom* with the intimate contemplation of the Gospel of St John, in which the holy spirit of Christ is embodied, we unite our spiritualized thinking with the past, present, and future stream of the Christ impulse.

We experience that this purified astral body, which bears within it at the moment of illumination none of the impure impressions of the physical world, forms in our soul the organs of perception of the spiritual world. As Rudolf Steiner says, it is called in esoteric Christianity 'the pure, chaste, wise "Virgin Sophia"'. The purified astral body, becoming Spirit Self, is the power which 'as Sophia encounters the cosmic Ego [the Christ], the universal Ego that causes illumination'. When the Christ Ego is individualized and dwells in the human heart, we experience how the cosmic Mother, Sophia, working through her son, Michael, serves the receiving and conceiving, individuation and recapitulation, of the given 'I'-copy of this cosmic Ego, in the second meeting with the Christ; then we can conceive the 'I' of the etheric Christ through the pure sunlight that radiates from her pure cosmic thinking and imagination. In this moment, we feel that we are 'surrounded by light, spiritual light. This second power that approaches the Virgin Sophia [the cosmic Ego of the Christ] is called in esoteric Christianity, and also today, "the Holy Spirit"'.[123] We experience that in this way, the indwelling Christ becomes the giver of the indwelling insight, the Holy Spirit, which today becomes the source of free human spiritual activity, the spirit light of modern spiritual science. Thus, we actualize in our hearts a mystery of far-reaching significance for the whole future evolution of humanity: the ages-long metamorphosis of cosmic Sophia, her human becoming through the given Ego of Christ and his Holy Spirit. Through the will of yoga of Michael, the light of cosmic Sophia is transformed and individualized in the human heart, and the cosmic being of the mother is metamorphosed through her son in the human heart. And she becomes the process of her living metamorphosis, as she completes in the present Age of Michael, her gradual descent from the cosmos to earth, from the highest spiritual hierarchies to humanity. And in the human soul and heart, individualizing the forces of the Christ and Michael, the culmination of this cosmic-human metamorphosis takes place today. We become her becoming, and experience her metamorphosis, becoming in us grandmother, mother, and granddaughter alike, when she is born as the being of purely human spiritual wisdom, *Anthropos-Sophia*.

As we showed above, the light of the Virgin Sophia is the light that illuminates the reception and individuation of the Ego of Christ. It is the light of the Holy Grail, that today is the light of true modern spiritual science. When the given 'I' is fully embodied, its indwelling insight becomes the light of the Grail. It reveals its source in Michael's activity, as the messenger of cosmic Sophia. When we research the concrete details of this process, we discover how it leads us, step by step, to the birth and meeting with Anthroposophia, that gradually takes on the form of a real supersensible

---

[123] Lecture of 31 May 1908 (GA 103) and 5 November 1906 (GA 94). When the purified astral body becomes Spirit Self and the etheric body begins to become Life Spirit, the inner connection between the Gospels of John and Luke is revealed. It is the connection between Virgin Sophia, Spirit Self, the transformed astral body, and the pure Adamic etheric forces of the virgin Nathanic forces, described in the lectures on the Gospel of St Luke (GA 114). The forces of Spirit Self and Life Spirit are necessary for the building of the *whole* bridge, including its third, spiritual-physical layer, described in the new edition of *The New Experience of the Supersensible*.

being. This birth process in the human soul and heart is a most intimate spiritual cognitive process. Let us use the first meditation that Rudolf Steiner gave in his fundamental book, *Knowledge of the Higher Worlds,* to describe this mystery more closely.

If man enters with all the forces of the Christ-given 'I' into pure thinking, he feels how 'he shifts the central point of his being to the inner part of his nature. He listens to the voices within him which speak to him in his moments of tranquillity; he cultivates an intercourse with the spiritual world.'

This intercourse assumes the form of a real dialogue, a conversation, with a hidden being that weaves through this pure thinking, but remains invisible, because to begin with we are totally immersed in the experience of pure thinking. The first real spiritual experience on this path occurs when we feel that we are now 'plunged in a world of thought'. This experience calls forth in the soul, in a natural way, 'a living feeling for this silent thought-activity'. And man feels how the deepest feelings of gratitude and devotion are aroused in his heart, as he learns 'to love what the spirit pours into him'.

This love is infinitely enhanced by the life forces flowing from the meeting with the Christ. This love gives substance and consistency to the weaving and flowing thoughts and converts them into real being; the pupil feels that 'he begins to deal with his thoughts as with things in space', and soon he would feel that this 'silent inward thought-work' flows into his soul from a world which is 'much higher, much more real, than the things in space'. He begins to sense the being that flows into him through these thoughts, as a real spiritual being, though he cannot yet perceive her as such with his inner light of seeing. If he lets his etheric heart be fired by the indwelling 'I' of Christ, a light will shine forth from the heart and illuminate his thinking. Then 'he discovers that something living expresses itself in this thought-world'; and the moment will arrive in which a most subtle, gentle, yet momentous event occurs, and he will experience that 'through his thoughts hidden beings speak to him, out of the silence, speech becomes audible to him'. This is the singular moment, described above from a different point of view, in which the indwelling insight of the indwelling 'I' is born in the human heart, and with it 'the flesh becomes Word', embodying the being of the self-conscious spiritual 'I'.

What was a thought dialogue and conversation with the flowing streams and currents of pure thoughts, becomes 'an inner language, an inner word', and man experiences the being of this pure thought so near and tangible, as never before. 'This moment, when first experienced, is one of greatest bliss for the student.' This bliss is not an ecstatic rapture into higher worlds, nor an intoxication that lowers and subdues our self-consciousness; on the contrary, in utmost stillness and tranquillity, the thinking 'I', *becomes* the inner word, and man feels himself transformed into a free spiritual being, possessing clear self-consciousness. Man is transformed into the likeness of the hidden being that unites with him through her inner word, and becoming one with this being, he experiences her world, that she experiences in him. Then this 'inner light' awakened in his soul, illuminates 'the whole external world', in which he finds his new home as a self-conscious spiritual being. In this way, 'a second life begins for him' and 'through his being pours a divine stream from a world of divine bliss'.[124]

This is an absolutely real experience that man can have today through the union and essence exchange between the impulses of Christ and Michael in the human heart, that gave birth to the indwelling 'I'. This union brings about the birth of a second spiritual offspring. This being lives and weaves constantly in and through our soul, supports and guides our spiritual life and illuminates our spiritual knowledge during these meetings and births; now we experience how this being herself, in her turn, becomes enlivened and irradiated by the forces flowing from Christ and Michael. Her spiritual grandmother, Sophia, who gave birth to the knowledge of the Christ through her son Michael, is revealed through the light of her son; through her son, she offered her light to illuminate the meetings with Christ and Michael and brought about their sacred union.

She had to wait until the development of the Consciousness Soul was strengthened by the new Christ forces, to give birth

---

[124] *Knowledge of the Higher Worlds*, Chapter 1: 'How to gain knowledge of the higher worlds' (GA 10). This intimate description of the birth and becoming process of Anthroposophia is possible thanks to the previous birth of the indwelling 'I' of Christ in the human 'I', illuminated by the light of the Holy Grail, the purified astral body, Virgin Sophia, kindled by *The Philosophy of Freedom*.

to the modern, fully human anthroposophical knowledge of the Christ, as the Goddess Isis gave birth to Horus and resurrected Osiris in the soul of the initiates in Ancient Egypt. Now the indwelling 'I' of Christ, born in this event, has become mature enough to face the cosmic grandmother; in turning to her, he lets the light that illuminated the reception and individuation of Christ's 'I'—a light that, as he knows now for the first time, he received from her—radiate back *to illuminate her.* When a ray of his resurrected Christ power illuminates her, she undergoes a metamorphosis, a new birth; she becomes younger again. She becomes a spiritual human being, following the path of Christ and Michael to the earth and human hearts. She stands now in the etheric world, unveiled and shining, as the true new Isis, enveloped by the light garment of the new, earthly-human sun. In this face-to-face meeting, we see our whole human being, imaginatively speaking, reflected to us, as it appears in the universe as an independent spiritual being, the wisdom and love-filled being of our true humanity: *Anthropos-Sophia.* And we see the divine-human gaze in her eyes, mysteriously revealing her-self as our-self, and when our gaze meets her powerful yet infinitely gentle gaze, it becomes her gaze.

Then we experience the mutual essence exchange between the indwelling 'I' and the indwelling being of Michael-Sophia, as she becomes Anthropos-Sophia; and in the face of this meeting, we say to ourselves: Now we can become free human-cosmic beings! Sophia became Anthropos-Sophia, born on earth through Michael and Rudolf Steiner; and the forces of pure thinking, of love in its spiritual form, that purified the astral body and transformed it into Spirit Self, Virgin Sophia, harbours her microcosmic human granddaughter. With her forces we could individualize the given meeting with Christ and enter a second time into the Grail Castle, to give birth to the indwelling 'I' in the human heart. When cosmic Sophia completes this task in the Age of Michael, she would become fully human, and take her place in the divine-human family in the etheric heart.

The spiritual being of Anthroposophia stands revealed before our inner gaze, when we gain a first-hand experience of what Rudolf Steiner meant when he said that 'it is not the Christ that we miss, but the knowledge of Christ, the Isis of Christ; the Sophia of Christ we miss ... What has caused the misfortune of civilized humanity in the new age is not the loss of the Christ, who stands before us in a higher glory than Osiris stood before the Egyptians... no, what we have lost is the knowledge, the sight of Jesus Christ. We must find it again by means of the power of Jesus Christ which is in us. The Christ will appear in the twentieth century in his spiritual form, not because something external will enter [into human evolution] but because human beings will find that power represented by the Holy Sophia'.[125]

And the union of the Christ with the human soul is accomplished when His 'I' is not only given as a gift of grace, but when it is also activity individualized, when it becomes an indwelling 'I' in the human 'I', through the free human individuation of Michael's will and activity. In this union, 'the Christ will transform us Himself and stream through us with His divine love life until we become as illumined and pure as He is, become like Him. Until He can share His divine consciousness with us our soul must become pure and wise through his light—then it can unite with his life. *This then is the union of Christ and Sophia, the union of Christ's life with the human soul* that has been purified by his light'.[126]

Sophia's pristine light that illuminates human evolution from the Alpha to the Omega, that became pure thinking as the being of *Philo-Sophia*, 'love in its spiritual form', becomes now a human-cosmic being, *the human being Anthropos-Sophia*. In this way we begin to individualize and recapitulate, in free human life and experience, the triple becoming process of Sophia: her mysterious path from the primordial heights of cosmic Sophia, through Philo-Sophia, to Anthroposophia, about which Rudolf Steiner could give only a very few indications at the beginning of the last century.

Through the meeting with Anthroposophia, we realize the significance of the meeting of Christ and Michael in the human heart. We realize what is brought about when the two sun streams of Christ and Michael, the streams of love and light, meet again in the human heart after they separated 2500 years ago. Rudolf Steiner opened this way for all modern people in *The Philosophy of Freedom* in 1894. He united for the first time, through his human deed of

---

[125] Lecture of 24 December 1920 (GA 202). And see also lecture of 10 February 1923 (GA 221).
[126] Esoteric lesson of 24 September 1907 (GA 266). My italics.

freedom and love, the light of cosmic wisdom and the love of cosmic life, divided between Michael and Christ when they separated. Through his free human deed of love, the cosmic intelligence ruled by Michael, the offspring of cosmic Sophia, after becoming human thinking in the being of Philo-Sophia, became fully human: *Anthroposophia* was born in her firstborn human being.[127] Since the end of the twentieth century, the path to Anthroposophia, that Rudolf Steiner opened for all humanity, could begin its actualization among ordinary, non-initiated people, inspired by the new revelation of the etheric Christ.

Naturally, we still lack the creative and formative spiritual forces to be able to form the adequate concepts and words, indeed, the language required to describe such mysteries, which are only in their very first budding beginnings. But this beginning must be accomplished in the present Age of Michael, because in this age seeds must be created and planted, the only source from which the future spiritual forces of humanity can develop.

In the light of what was described thus far, I believe that we can begin to understand the mysterious indications of Rudolf Steiner concerning the being of Anthroposophia, not with our dead thoughts, but with the living thinking of our etheric hearts. 'How then does the Consciousness Soul confront Sophia? This is done so that it brings the "I" into direct relationship with Sophia.' This was described above, when we showed how the human 'I' is impregnated by the 'I' of Christ, and how this seed is individualized, nourished, and fostered by the forces of love in its spiritual form, begotten by the spiritualized thinking of *The Philosophy of Freedom*. Then we demonstrated how 'the activity of the "I" within the relationship between the Consciousness Soul and Sophia', brings it about that 'Sophia... will take with her what humanity is'; that is, Sophia will take with her humanity in so far as the human soul has received the seed of Christ's 'I' and individualized it into the indwelling 'I' through Michael, with the forces of the Consciousness Soul. Then 'she will present herself not only as Sophia, but as Anthroposophia', and 'after passing through the human soul, through the very being of the human being', she will 'henceforth bear that being within her, and in this form she will confront

---

[127] I described the spiritual being of Rudolf Steiner and his current activity, in the third lecture of the *Twilight and Resurrection of Humanity*,

enlightened human beings as the objective being Sophia who once stood before the Greeks'.[128]

This is the objective spiritual meeting with the presently developing cosmic being of humanity, revealed for the first time on earth in the new Age of Michael. The pristine cosmic spirit light of Sophia, working through Michael, leads our imaginative cognition to the Christ, and thanks to her we can individualize the gift of His 'I'; then we can rightly feel how 'Christ gives us our humanity' and how the being of Sophia becomes Anthroposophia, and reveals to us our true humanity. Then the essence exchanges between the four individualized spiritual beings and their interrelationships in the etheric heart, lights up in all its beauty and splendour in the human soul:

> The primeval Light [of cosmic Sophia] appears again in the Light brought by Christ to the human Ego. In the life in union with Christ this blissful thought may shine like a sun through the whole soul: 'The glorious primal Divine Light is here again; it shines... and man unites himself, while in the present, with the spiritual, cosmic forces of Light belonging to that past when he was not yet a free individual. And in this Light he can find the paths which lead him aright as a human being, when in his soul he unites himself, with understanding, with the Michael Mission... certainty of soul and spirit flourishes... through which he will be able to traverse the cosmic path upon which he will, without losing his origin, in the future find his true perfection.'[129]

Historically, the birth of Anthroposophia, the birth of the universal spiritual being of humanity, was conceived and demonstrated through Rudolf Steiner in the Christmas Foundation Conference of 1923-4. In this event, he demonstrated the entire becoming, birth and developmental process of the cosmic human being Anthroposophia, in body, soul and spirit, connected to the nine hierarchies, the divine trinity and the Christ impulse. Once human beings will

---

[128] The only lecture about the triple mystery of Sophia, Philosophia and Anthroposophia, was given on 3 February, 1913, during the first General Meeting of the newly founded Anthroposophical Society. See *The Effects of Esoteric Development*, Anthroposophic Press, 1977, pp. 13-16.

[129] *Leading Thoughts*, 'The Mission of Michael in the Cosmic Age of Human Freedom' (GA 26).

receive this seed into their etheric hearts in the twenty-first century, fructified by the new etheric impulses of Christ and Michael, they 'will learn how profoundly what anthroposophy gives us is based in our whole being', because they will truly experience that 'we receive through anthroposophy our very own being... it is the essence of anthroposophy that its own being consists of the being of the human... we receive from anthroposophy what we ourselves are and what we must place before ourselves, because we must practice self-knowledge'.[130]

But this requires that 'Anthroposophy itself is seen as a living, supersensible, invisible being who moves among us... as the invisible being of Anthroposophia... it requires a sense of alliance in every living moment with the invisible being of Anthroposophia'.[131] What the knowledge drama of the Second Coming brings to full consciousness is 'the fact that Anthroposophia is something that proceeds from us, shines forth from us, springs forth and blossoms out of our noblest forces. We need to draw attention to this quite explicitly. We cannot leave it unsaid.'[132]

Above we described what is meant by 'our noblest forces', produced in the etheric essence exchange between the forces of the Christ, Michael, Sophia and Philosophia, actualized by the self-conscious spiritual 'I' in the Consciousness Soul. Then we experience, in all reality, that 'Anthroposophy is a human being in herself. If she was not a human being, she couldn't transform us. She makes us into another human being. She is a human being herself; I say this in a serious sense. Anthroposophy is not a teaching, Anthroposophy is something real, she is a human being.'

We saw that the indwelling 'I' of Christ in the human 'I' makes us into self-conscious spiritual beings in the Age of Michael, in which spiritualized thinking, born out of *The Philosophy of Freedom*, spiritualizes the Consciousness Soul and transforms it into the Imaginative Soul, the burgeoning Spirit Self. And with this Imaginative Soul we perceive our innermost cosmic-human being also objectively in the etheric world, together with the beings of Christ and Michael. Then we feel that 'our personality is wholly penetrated by her, and we experience Anthroposophy as a human being, that

[130] Lecture of 3 February 1913, Berlin (unpublished).
[131] Lecture of 17 June 1923 (GA 258).
[132] Lecture of 26 March 1922 (GA 211).

thinks, but also feels, senses, and has will impulses, when Anthroposophy thinks, feels and wills in us, when she really becomes a whole human being, then we can grasp her, then we have her. She works like a being, and she enters like a kind of being into the present civilization and culture.'[133] This imaginative vision becomes objective, as the innermost essence of the human soul is revealed in the etheric world through the imagination of Anthroposophia.

'The human being Anthroposophia' is, therefore, the sister of the divine-human child born of the marriage of Christ and Sophia, officiated by Michael, as the high priest of Christ, actualized through the deeds of freedom and love inspired by *The Philosophy of Freedom*. We participate in this marriage, because the indwelling 'I' of Christ, active in our spiritualized 'I', is the elder brother of Anthroposophia, and both live together creatively and joyfully in so far as we make freedom and love real in our physical life. As Rudolf Steiner said to W. J. Stein in The Hague in 1922, 'Anthroposophia is a human being. She is *that* human being, created out of the deed of freedom.'[134]

In the etheric heart and world, the three beings, Christ, Michael and Anthroposophia, are most intimately connected with each other, united through the indwelling 'I'. They are living, weaving, and pulsating, in perpetual essence exchange of their spiritual forces, in the above-described processes of etheric breathing. With the etheric heart organ formed in Michaelic Yoga, we perceive how Michael's and Christ's enhanced life through each other, reveal the secret of their being and becoming in the indwelling 'I'; we perceive how the etheric breathing of the Christ in and through Michael, and the etheric breathing of Michael in and through the Christ, give birth to the being of universal humanity, Anthroposophia.

And the living being of Anthroposophia illuminates and enhances, with Sophia's light of spirit knowledge, the reciprocal etheric weaving of Christ and Michael in the etheric hearts of men and in the etheric earthly-human sun. Through this triple essence exchange through the indwelling 'I', we unveil the veiled secret

---

[133] Lecture of 29 September 1921 (GA 343).

[134] *Das 'Haager Gespräch', W. J Stein-Rudolf Steiner, Dokumentation eines wegweisenden Zusammenwirkens* (Verlag am Goetheanum, 1985) p. 299. Italics in original.

of the new Isis: *the etheric reality of world-man in the man-created, Christ-permeated world. In the indwelling 'I' of Christ, the Conscious-ness Soul's child of Michael, the human being Anthropos-Sophia is born, bearing and nourishing the future Earthly-Human Sun in her heart.* This unveiled being is the 'open secret' of the modern mystery of the resurrected Isis, the spiritual being of Anthropos-Sophia.[135]

Philosophically expressed, this secret is formulated by Rudolf Steiner thus:

> Such a way of knowledge can be termed anthroposophical, and the knowledge of reality gained by it is Anthroposophy, because it must take its departure from the fact that the truly real man (Anthropos) lies hidden behind what is revealed by the knowledge of nature and what is found in the inner life of ordinary consciousness. In obscure feeling, in the unconscious soul life, this truly real man expresses himself; through anthro-posophical research it will be lifted into consciousness.[136]

This 'truly, real man' is the one referred to also in *The Philosophy of Freedom* as the man-world being, that cancels the subject-object dualism of ordinary consciousness and unites itself again with the cosmos in full self-consciousness:

> In that we sense and feel (and perceive), we are single beings; in that we think, we are the *all-one being that penetrates everything*.[137]

And in the book *Mysticism at the Dawn of the Modern Age*:

> I live, therefore, a double life, the life of a thing among things, which lives in its body and perceives by means of its organs what takes place outside this body; and above this life a higher one, which is not limited by such inner and outer, which reaches across and extends beyond the external world and itself. There-fore, I would have to say: first I am an individual, limited 'I'; then, secondly, *I am a general, universal 'I'*.[138]

---

[135] *The Search for the New Isis, Divine Sophia*, lectures of 23-26 December 1920 (GA 202).
[136] *Philosophy and Anthroposophy* (GA 35).
[137] *The Philosophy of Freedom*, Chapter 5 (GA 4). My italics.
[138] *Mysticism at the Dawn of the Modern Age*, Preface (GA 7). My italics.

The loftiest region of the eternal union between the cosmic beings of Christ and Sophia is beyond the higher Devachan, in the Buddhi sphere, or world of macrocosmic archetypes (*Ur-Bilder Welt*), where also the twelve Bodhisattvas are gathered around the Christ. The task of the twelve is to reflect, as a Sophian light of wisdom and knowledge, the living stream of Christ's appearance, words and deeds. This spirit light of wisdom is the Holy Spirit in its macro-cosmic form.[139] This is also the realm from which flow the primary spirit forces that form the new, Christ-given, imaginative faculties of humanity.[140]

Anthroposophical spiritual science, therefore, actualizes on the earth in modern self-consciousness, a spiritual mission that until this age could only be accomplished in the highest spiritual world. 'So we feel ourselves standing, in full understanding, in the coming together of two streams of world conception. The one should bring us a deepened conception of the Christ problem, the Mystery of Golgotha, and the other should bring us new concepts and ideas about reality. The two must flow together in our time. This will not be possible without the worst hindrances.'[141]

This fully modern and creative connection formed between Anthroposophia, the new Holy Spirit, and the Christ, is possible because 'the Holy Spirit is the great teacher of those whom we call the Masters of Wisdom and the Harmony of Feelings... what is brought forth as wisdom through the spiritual scientific move-ment, in order to understand the world and its spirits, *flows through the Holy Spirit into the Lodge of the Twelve, and this is that which will, eventually, bring humanity to a self-conscious, free understanding of Christ and the event of Golgotha*'.[142]

This means, in other words, that the anthroposophical knowl-edge of the Christ is a new, free spiritual creation of the age of the Consciousness Soul, which streams, for the first time, as a new stream of the Holy Spirit, *from the Earth upwards* to the high-est Buddhi plane. Or, in other words, it is the first realization of the Holy Spirit in the new, Christed Earthly-Human Sun sphere,

---

[139] Lectures of 31 August 1919 (GA 113), 25 October 1909 (GA 116), 6 Sep-tember 1910 (GA 123), and 9 January 1912 (GA 130).

[140] Lecture of 28 March 1910 (GA 119).

[141] Lecture of 13 March 1911 (GA 124).

[142] Lecture of 22 March 1909 (GA 107). My italics.

in which Christ has established His new Earth and Heaven, and around which the new circle of the new teachers of humanity is formed.[143]

The human-cosmic being of Anthroposophia incarnated for the first—very short—time in the laying of the Foundation Stone of future humanity in the Christmas Foundation Conference. It was embodied until the death of Rudolf Steiner on 30 March 1925. In his soul and heart, it became the 'individually free human being within the reigning work of the gods in the cosmos, as *a cosmic human being, an individual human being within the cosmic human being*'.[144] Before and after his death, this being continuously 'knocks on the portal of our hearts and says: Let me in, because I am your true self; I am your true humanity!' And this being, 'that really knocks on our hearts in order to give us our true being, to give us ourselves... to bring into us what again can find the way out as true human love to the other person; because when we let Anthroposophy enter into our hearts, after she touched them, then Anthroposophy will bring us, through what she is, true human love'.[145]

Yet even after a century and a half of the present Age of Michael has passed, human beings still forcefully harden their hearts and push this being—their true self—away; they stubbornly continue to close their hearts and prevent their true humanity from entering, and the descent of humanity into the abyss deepens with each day. And true spiritual science has since 1923-4 one central task: to prepare enough human souls and hearts to receive and individualize the second incarnation of Anthroposophia in this century. This task must be fulfilled in the present Age of Michael, to build a human community, in which free human hearts unite in true human love, in living and growing brotherhood and sisterhood, in which Anthroposophia will be able to incarnate and live again, to try and remain longer on earth than was possible in her shortest previous incarnation. But this can only happen if she finds open

---

[143] About the Masters in the Eastern and Western esoteric streams, see GA 264. This modern cultus of humanity, taking place in the sun temple of the earthly-human sun, is described in the new edition of *The New Experience of the Supersensible*.

[144] Laying of the Foundation Stone of the new Anthroposophical Society, 25 December 1923 (GA 260).

[145] Address to the members of the Anthroposophical Society in Holland, after the lecture of 18 November 1923 (GA 231, p. 154).

and welcoming etheric hearts and deeds of true love, done by her fellow human beings, working and striving together in love and harmony:

> And if you hear this resounding in your own hearts, my dear friends, then what you will establish here will be a true union of human beings on behalf of *Anthroposophia* and will carry the spirit which prevails in radiant thought-light around our dodecahedral stone of love out into the world, where it may shed light and warmth on the progress of human souls and the progress of the world.[146]

---

[146] Laying of the Foundation Stone, ibid.

Quoted volumes from Rudolf Steiner's Collected Works

English titles are given where translations are available.

CW 3	*Truth and Knowledge.* Also: *Truth and Science*
CW 4	*The Philosophy of Freedom.* Also: *Intuitive Thinking as a Spiritual Path* and *The Philosophy of Freedom as Spiritual Activity*
CW 7	*Mystics at the Dawn of the Modern Age*
CW 10	*Knowledge of the Higher Worlds.* Also: *How to Know Higher Worlds*
CW 13	*Occult Science, An Outline Outline.* Also: *Esoteric Science*
CW 16/17	*A Way of Self-Knowledge and the Threshold of the Spiritual World*
CW 21	*The Riddles of the Soul*
CW 24	*Renewal of the Social Organism*
CW 26	*Anthroposophical Leading Thoughts*
CW 35	*Philosophie und Anthroposophie: Gesammelte Aufsätze 1904-1923* ('Philosophy and Anthroposophy: Collected Essays 1904-1923')
CW 40	*Truth-Wrought Words*
CW 73	*Anthroposophy Has Something to Add to Modern Sciences*
CW 74	*The Redemption of Thinking*
CW 89	*Awareness – Life – Form*
CW 94	*An Esoteric Cosmology*
CW 103	*The Gospel of St John*
CW 107	*Disease, Karma, and Healing*
CW 109/111	*The Principle of Spiritual Economy*
CW 112	*The Gospel of St John and Its Relation to the Other Gospels*
CW 113	*The East in the Light of the West*
CW 116	*The Christ Impulse*

CW 219   *Man and the World of Stars*

CW 220   *Awake! For the Sake of the Future*

CW 221   *Earthly Knowledge and Heavenly Wisdom*

CW 231   *At Home in the Universe*

CW 232   *Mystery Knowledge and Mystery Centres*

CW 233   *World History in the Light of Anthroposophy*

CW 233a   *Rosicrucianism and Modern Initiation*

CW 237   *Karmic Relationships, Vol. 3*

CW 238   *Karmic Relationships, Vol. 4*

CW 240   *Karmic Relationships, Vol. 6*

CW 243   *True and False Paths in Spiritual Investigation*

CW 258   *The Anthroposophic Movement*

CW 260   *The Christmas Conference for the Founding of the General Anthroposophical Society 1923/1924*

CW 264   *From the History and the Contents of the First Section of the Esoteric School*

CW 266/1   *Esoteric Lessons 1904-1909*

CW 266/2   *Esoteric Lessons 1910-1912*

CW 266/3   *Esoteric Lessons 1913 -1923*

CW 270   *Esoteric Lessons for the First Class of the School of Spiritual Science at the Goetheanum*

CW 322   *The Boundaries of Natural Science*

CW 343   *Vorträge und Kurse über christlich-religiöses Wirken, Bd.2 Spirituelles Erkennen – Religiöses Empfinden – Kultisches Handeln* ('Lectures and Courses on Christian Religious Work, Vol. 2: Spirit Knowing – Religious Feeling – Cultic Doing')

CW 346   *The Book of Revelation and the Work of the Priest*

For English-language titles contact Rudolf Steiner Press, UK (www.rudolf-steinerpress.com) or SteinerBooks, USA (www.steinerbooks.org)

A note from the publisher

For more than a quarter of a century, **Temple Lodge Publishing** has made available new thought, ideas and research in the field of spiritual science.

Anthroposophy, as founded by Rudolf Steiner (1861-1925), is commonly known today through its practical applications, principally in education (Steiner-Waldorf schools) and agriculture (biodynamic food and wine). But behind this outer activity stands the core discipline of spiritual science, which continues to be developed and updated. True science can never be static and anthroposophy is living knowledge.

Our list features some of the best contemporary spiritual-scientific work available today, as well as introductory titles. So, visit us online at **www.templelodge.com** and join our emailing list for news on new titles.

If you feel like supporting our work, you can do so by buying our books or making a direct donation (we are a non-profit/ charitable organisation).

office@templelodge.com

※ TEMPLE LODGE

For the finest books of Science and Spirit